michael bublé onstage offstage

PHOTOGRAPHY AND CREATIVE DIRECTION BY DEAN FREEMAN

G

GALLERY BOOKS

New York

London

Toronto

Sydney

New Delhi

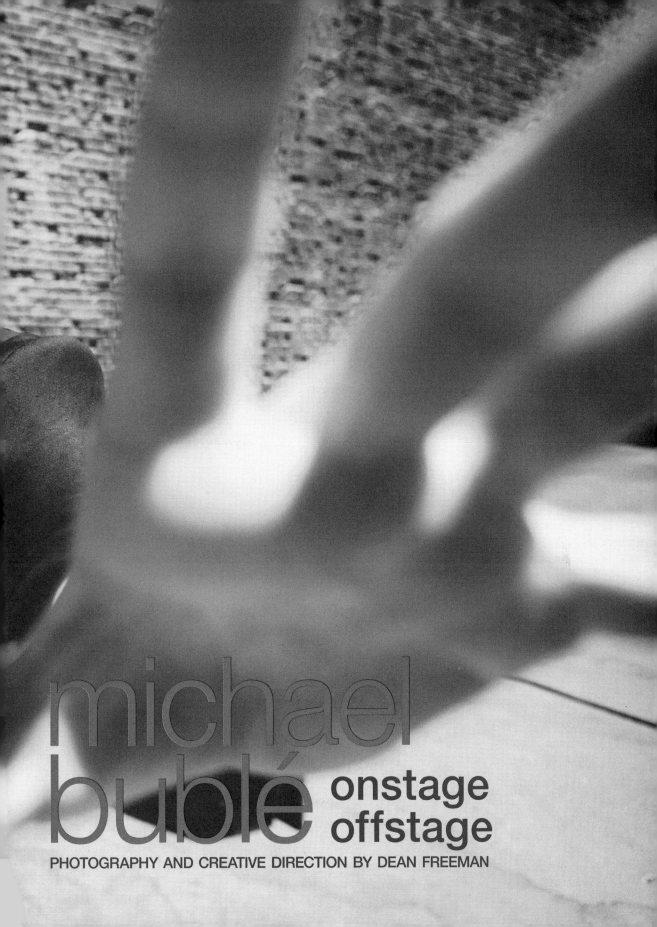

michael bublé onstage offstage

PHOTOGRAPHY AND CREATIVE DIRECTION BY DEAN FREEMAN

Gallery Books
A Division of Simon & Schuster, Inc.
1230 Avenue of the Americas
New York, NY 10020

Design by Joby Ellis

Originally published in Great Britain by Bantam Press

First Gallery Books hardcover edition November 2011

GALLERY BOOKS and colophon are registered trademarks
of Simon & Schuster, Inc.

For information about special discounts for bulk purchases, please contact Simon
& Schuster Special Sales at 1-866-506-1949 or business@simonandschuster.com

The Simon & Schuster Speakers Bureau can bring authors to your live event. For
more information or to book an event contact the Simon & Schuster Speakers
Bureau at 1-866-248-3049 or visit our website at www.simonspeakers.com.

Manufactured in the United States of America

1 3 5 7 9 10 8 6 4 2

Library of Congress Cataloging-in-Publication Data is available.

ISBN 978-1-4516-7471-2

contents

born
to
sing

In near darkness, I am standing backstage and a sound guy is shoving a microphone pack down the back of my pants. My assistant is straightening my tie, tucking in my shirt. The staircase to the stage is before me, my band is assembled and waiting on that stage, and beyond that are fifteen thousand or so people who've paid their hard-earned cash to see me perform.

In that moment I am enveloped with a strange sense of focus and calm.

It may seem counter-intuitive to feel peaceful just before going onstage in front of fifteen thousand people. But for me, it is sheer bliss.

They tell me I have sold 27 million records worldwide, and I was among the top five biggest grossing North American touring acts of 2010, along with veterans Bon Jovi, Roger Waters, the Dave Matthews Band and the Eagles.

Those numbers are nice because they tell me I'm doing something right. But it's at that moment when I'm about to climb those stairs and go on to the stage, feeling the audience's anticipation and my own anxiety that I'll do a good job for them, that I feel the most gratitude. It's when all is right in my world because all I ever wanted to be was a performer. I wanted it so badly that, to me, this chaotic, insanely busy and structured life I'm living – flying from country to country, playing one tour date after another, sometimes around 150 shows a year – makes wonderfully perfect sense.

The journey from singing into a hairbrush in my suburban Canadian bedroom to singing onstage at New York's Madison Square Garden was a much longer one than most people will realize. I'm young, still in my mid-thirties, but I started performing when I was too young to drink and shouldn't even have been allowed in nightclubs. I was also young and naïve enough to think that making it was easily within my grasp. I was wrong. I had to work, beg, and charm my way on to that stage, with the help of a group of people who came to believe in me, even when I didn't totally believe in myself.

It all began when I was a little kid, when I learned my family's address. My father taught me to sing it, because he knew that by singing it, I'd remember it. I'll never forget the little tune I composed to sing those four numbers and the name of the quiet street where I grew up in Burnaby, British Columbia. That little song was my first foray into music, and it came to me as naturally as shooting a hockey puck.

My maternal grandfather, Mitch Santaga, was responsible for introducing me to the old American standards, usually sung by Italian immigrants like my own family – crooners like Tony Bennett, Frank Sinatra and Dean Martin. I think you could definitely make the link between Italians and this kind of music. With Italian families, there is genuine warmth and a lot of love, tactile, hands-on love. We love our family, our food and our music.

Grandpa Mitch loved those old singers, and he taught me to love them, too. I spent a lot of time hanging around my grandpa because we're a family who love each other's company. Let's just say that, at Christmas time, nobody's dreading the holidays. I love Christmas because it is precisely all about family. My family sustains me. I couldn't have achieved any kind of success without their love and support. They shaped me into the man I am today, and if I should ever lose sight of that, they'd be the first people to kick my butt into shape. That's important, because I've achieved enough success that people aren't always upfront with me any more. They tend to agree with every idea that comes out of my mouth, and I don't hear the word 'no' so much.

Being famous has the double-pronged reality that everybody will listen to your stories and laugh whether or not they find you funny. That kind of thing can be a hindrance to your growth as an artist. I don't have to mention the names of talented performers who've lost their path in life as they became more famous. We know who they are, and I have a strong suspicion that part of the problem was that people either stopped levelling with them, or they stopped listening. My family, on the other hand, is my trusted judge and jury, and I will listen to them as I have all my life. My mom, Amber, for example, has no problem telling me if I'm being crude and lewd, which isn't entirely unnatural for me. Anyone who's caught my show will know about my propensity for the *risqué* and dark side of comedy. If I take it too far, though, my mom will phone me up. 'Michael, did you really need to say that?' she'll ask, in the disappointed tone that kept me in line as a kid.

When I was growing up, she was the perfect blend: a mother I was afraid of, who was also a great guiding presence for my two sisters and me. It was a healthy fear. And she didn't cross the line like some parents do and become our best buddy. Who needs another buddy? We needed a mom. She was a disciplinarian. You didn't mess around. She was a good, fun young mom, but she could put me in my place with one look.

And I wasn't an easy kid to raise, believe me. One time a reporter asked me what terrible things I'd got up to as a kid. What didn't I do? I was a jerk. I went through some bad times, especially in my teens. I was fighting a lot. I was really angry. I was insecure and I think I took it out on the people who loved me most, as many of us do. When we're not feeling great, we hurt the ones we love.

I don't have kids yet, but I know that I'll raise them like my parents raised me – by being strict, loving and hopelessly devoted. Kids need boundaries to make them feel safe. But I'm skipping ahead of myself here. Let me tell you more about my upbringing, because it explains everything that I am today, not just professionally but as a person.

My dad worked as a commercial salmon fisherman and my mom stayed at home to raise my younger sisters, Crystal and Brandee, and me. Our house was boisterous and at times loud, compared to my friends' homes, which might not be too surprising, considering our Italian heritage.

I contributed to the chaos by fulfilling my cliché role as the big brother who tormented his little sisters. To this day, I still call Crystal 'Joe' because I caught her kissing a kid named Joey when she was five or six. Oh, that was a beautiful moment for me because I had new ammunition. 'Joey, Joey, Joey,' I'd taunt her. She'd go crazy.

When my parents would leave me to babysit, I'd tell Crystal or Brandee to put on my big padded hockey pants and play goalie so I could practise shooting pucks off them. I was obsessed with hockey, my second greatest passion next to music. Being the human target could be a terrifying game for a small child, but I was an evil big brother. If they didn't obey me, I'd threaten to take them downstairs to the basement and put their little hands on the hot-water pipes. Then if they put on the hockey pants, which were way too big for them, I'd hold them down on the floor until they got claustrophobic and screamed their heads off. I'd sing, 'Sleepy time, sleepy time, it's sleepy time in the city.' I drove them crazy.

Of course, once I got old enough to like girls, I'd hang out with my sisters so I could talk to their friends. They both had gorgeous girlfriends who wanted nothing to do with a chunky fourteen-year-old nerd.

I had the typical boy's bedroom, with a Spider-Man poster and tons of *Star Wars* toys and decorations, like a Darth Vader light switch. I can't tell you how many times I sat at my desk at school and concentrated as hard as I possibly could, trying to move the pencil using 'the Force'. It never worked.

born to sing

Even today, in interviews, I'll often sneak a *Star Wars* reference into a quote, usually unbeknown to the reporters. When my bedroom was moved to the basement, my interest shifted from *Star Wars* to girlie magazines, which I kept in a secret panel in the ceiling.

A huge part of my childhood was devoted to my grandparents. They played as big a role in my life as my mother and father, which is fairly typical of Italian immigrant families. My grandparents are second-generation Italians, descending on my mother's side from a town outside Pescara, on the east coast of Italy. My grandpa Mitch Santaga's family came to work in the mines in Alberta, where he grew up as a farm boy in a tiny town called Saunders. My dad's father Frank was born in Vancouver, and his side of the family is from Dalmatia, originally Italian territory that became part of Yugoslavia after the Second World War. On that side of the family, some say we're Yugoslavian, others that we're Italian. Both my grandmothers are of Italian descent as well, but were born in Vancouver.

As for speaking Italian, I know some words and phrases, but I'm not fluent. My grandparents, as second-generation Italians, are more Italian than the Italians in Italy. Because they left the old country so long ago, they have preserved the old ways and traditions, and passed them down to us. That's why we share a love of music, food and family.

I was close to both my grandpas, but they couldn't have been more different. When I was little and too young to get a job, I'd spend every day of my summer holidays with my grandpa Mitch. I'd go to his house and listen to old records on his 1970s-era RCA console, lying on the green carpet in his living room. He'd play Vaughn Monroe's version of '(Ghost) Riders In The Sky', which would send shivers down my spine: it's a song about steel-hoofed cattle being chased across the sky by the spirits of cowboys damned to hell.

It was during those days and nights at my grandpa's house that my creative imagination developed. We'd sleep out under the stars on his back deck. He'd tell me the bears were going to get me and really freak me out. I was terrified in the way that little boys love to be terrified. He'd also pretend he could see Indian smoke signals in the distance. We were like cowboys on the range, lying there in our sleeping bags. I loved it.

Grandpa Mitch is a lovable, warm grandpa. Grandpa Frank, who died about a decade ago, was a lovable but irascible character, nicknamed 'the General'. He worked his whole life as captain of a fishing boat but never learned to swim. In summer, he'd walk around in his shorts, black dress socks up to his knees, with black penny loafers. And he loved Dolly Parton.

One time, he heard that the heavyweight boxing champion George Foreman was in Vancouver, and he was meeting fans. My grandpa admired Foreman. He had heard that Foreman liked salmon a lot so, being a fisherman, he brought along a case of salmon he'd canned himself. He waited for hours in a line-up to meet the legendary fighter, and when he got to the front, he handed him the salmon. Foreman was thrilled. My grandpa explained that he was a fisherman and had heard he liked salmon so had brought him a present. Foreman said something like, 'Gee, Frank, that's really sweet of you. Let me sign something for you.' And my grandpa said, 'I don't want your bloody autograph. Why the hell would I want that? Enjoy the salmon.' With that, he walked off. That was my grandpa Frank.

It was my grandpa Mitch who loved music. He would bring out his Mills Brothers or Brook Benton records, and we'd play them, old vinyl records that would hiss and skip. I sat surrounded by them. When I heard those golden voices, it was like I'd entered a place in time that made more sense to me than any of the contemporary songs my friends were listening to. Sure, I liked the bands that were big when I was a teenager, Guns 'N Roses and Metallica, but I idolized the way the old-time singers could phrase a few poignant words so that they stayed with you long after the music had stopped playing. It was my first understanding of what it meant to make great art, which is to capture a feeling, be it the bitter pain of despair or the sweet bliss of being in love. And they did it with such style, too. This wasn't sloppy sentimentalism. This was straight-up delivery, and those guys could swing. My grandpa's passion for that music kick-started my own, and it has bonded us for life. We had our secret fraternity for music nerds, and he loved having a grandson who shared his enjoyment and gobbled up his knowledge of old-time swing music.

To this day, if I go to his house, my grandfather will most likely be sitting cross-legged on the floor of his brick-walled living room, making cassette tapes of his old records. He'll make tapes of my music now, too. He just loves music. I bought him an iPod and he can't figure the thing out, but he thinks it's amazing. I give him credit for instilling in me everything I know and love about music.

Unlike a lot of performers, my career journey has not been solitary. My family has been with me every step of the way. It's basically been a joint project. For example, when I was making *Crazy Love*, my fourth album, my grandpa Mitch, grandma Yolanda, mom, dad, two sisters, their husbands and kids hung out for the day and watched me record multiple takes of the 'Stardust' track. It was my niece Jade's birthday, so my mom brought along a big chocolate cake, my grandma Yolanda made her traditional lasagne, and my grandpa brought his home-made wine. Having them there, in Bryan Adams's Warehouse Studio in Vancouver, was like a typical Sunday in our household, filled with food and banter.

Every so often that day I'd look through the glass and see my grandpa Mitch sitting there, moving his lips to the lyrics he knew so well. 'Stardust', recorded by Bing Crosby and everybody else back in the day, is one of his favourite old tunes. The pride on his face was unmistakable. My whole family sat there watching me with that look. It filled me with such love to see them there for me, supporting me with their presence, the way they have all my life. It made me feel like I was at home, not in a recording studio surrounded by techies and equipment. My family has been part of every record I've made, every tour I've done. My touring crew, which is about seventy strong, is accustomed to seeing them backstage, hanging out. My dad is my financial manager. I'm serious when I say that this is a joint effort. To my family, I'll always be their little guy, the kid who used to perform for them on the karaoke machine in the living room.

I come from a long line of fishermen, working-class men who worked hard and devoted themselves to family. They're macho Italian men, and they're proud of what they've earned. But they're not men who are afraid to show their emotions. As soon as I finished 'Stardust', I rushed into the room and grabbed my grandpa's face between both hands. He put his arm around me and his eyes were moist: 'This life you have, Michael, it's crazy. Crazy.'

If I ever need a reminder of what I've accomplished, all I have to do is look at my grandpa's face when I'm singing. The only difference now is that we might not be sitting in his living room listening to the old RCA. Now, we're just as likely to be in a fancy recording studio or backstage at Madison Square Garden.

My grandpa will sit in the studio for hours while I record, and he'll fly halfway around the world to watch me perform – even though he's in his eighties. You'd think a twenty-two-hour flight from Vancouver to Australia might be daunting for a guy of that age, but my grandpa travels like that regularly just to spend time with me.

It thrills me that I can make it happen for him because he wanted to be a singer, too: I'm living our dream. I like to tell audiences how my grandpa Mitch was a plumber who'd give musicians free plumbing service if they'd let me sing with them. While other kids were at the mall, I was in some cheesy hotel lounge singing with guys three times my age. That's just one small example of the effort my grandpa made on my behalf. He also accompanied me to auditions and talent shows.

Anyone who thinks the journey to showbiz success is hard and arduous is damn right. I was such a cocky kid, so sure of my abilities when I got out of that starting gate. I'd never have known it would take nearly a decade of work and determination – and moments of despair so bad that at times I thought of packing it in.

It's a cliché, but it holds true: you simply have to pay your dues in this world. Canadian writer Malcolm Gladwell theorizes that it takes 10,000 hours of hard work before anybody – Mozart, the Beatles, Bill Gates – achieves success in their field. I firmly agree. It doesn't matter how innately talented or gifted you are, you have to work, and you have to work hard, before you earn the right to sit back and say, 'I made it.'

And, for the record, I'm still not there.

Aside from a happy family, there are other childhood factors that define me now. Burnaby, where I grew up, is a sprawling suburb that butts up against the port city of Vancouver. There is a big Italian community, with lots of Italian restaurants, grocery stores and coffee shops, where old guys sit around and drink coffee for hours. I lived there my whole childhood, and I'm still connected to the place.

I had my demons. My childhood wasn't all sunshine and lollipops. In high school, I felt like a lot of different people. I wasn't part of the super-cool popular crowd, and even though I loved sports, I wasn't a jock. I don't recall having a steady girlfriend. I wasn't much of a student, but I was competitive as hell. One time there was this kid in the English class who told me I was stupid and he would do better than me. I made it my mission that year to get an A in English, just so I could beat him.

Meanwhile, I got a D in the easier food-management class because I was so busy chatting up the girls. I don't want to imply that I was a big hit with them, because I wasn't. I was a dork who couldn't hang on to a girlfriend for much longer than a week. I was also an unruly kid who had a knack for getting into trouble. One time I went on a class field trip to a bread factory and stole some bread because I thought it was funny. I was banned from future field trips. My mother was not pleased.

What can I say? I liked to stir things up. It took music to focus me.

The nice thing is that I'm still close to many of the kids from back then. I'm still close to my friend Carsten, who grew up on my street. I have a photo of him and me when we're five years old, and we're holding my new baby sister Crystal, who'd just come home from the hospital. Our street was filled with kids, and their parents were so much a part of our lives we'd refer to them as 'Aunt this' or 'Uncle that'. We grew up slow — we had a proper childhood filled with road hockey, gunfights, kick the can, chasing ice-cream trucks and building tree forts. We hung out at each other's houses, a whole group of kids all roughly the same age. I remember I had a crush on Dana Dong. My first kiss was with a girl named Jennifer Kiss, appropriately enough. She was my friend and she offered to teach me how to kiss. I had a secret crush on her so I was thrilled. But after we'd kissed, she said it'd felt like she was kissing her brother, which so destroyed me that I remember those words to this day.

When I was between eleven and fourteen years old, I wanted to be an actor, so I pushed my parents to take me to auditions for movie parts. I did a lot of community theatre outside high school. Although I suffered from stage fright, I put myself through those intensely nerve-racking auditions. But once I'd discovered the force that is Harry Connick Jr, I knew I wanted to be a singer.

Musically, Bing Crosby's *Merry Christmas* album had an enormous impact on me. It is the quintessential record. I hope to achieve a fraction of that classic sound with my own Christmas album one day. As a kid, I sang every one of those goddamn songs on that Crosby record. I was singing 'Mele Kalikimaka' come July. The arrangements are gorgeous and swinging, and Crosby's voice is beautiful. I just fell in love with it immediately. I loved Christmas because of the emotional attachment it had for me, and now there are memories of family and good times. For me, it was sheer perfection for Crosby to mix that feeling with the beautiful melodies and instrumentation.

Let's face it, I was a weird kid. What other kid would find an old Christmas record so exciting?

I knew I could sing. I used to sing a lot with my buddies. My friend Brad would say, 'You're singing with your fake voice,' because I'd use vibrato. They'd say, 'Shut up, Bublé.'

But then, of course, I found Harry Connick Jr. I can't remember where I heard him first, but I knew I'd fallen in love with the song 'It Had to Be You'. I really enjoyed his voice and realized I could emulate him. I started doing Harry Connick Jr impersonations at school, and I'd make everybody laugh. I also did a mean Christian Slater impersonation. More importantly, Connick taught me that I could sing with my own style. I didn't have to use vibrato or funny voices; instead, I could sing with authority, like a pro. It made me realize I was more of a singer than an actor, and that I wasn't just any kind of singer. My voice doesn't sound like every voice. If I wanted to sing hard rock, for example, I couldn't, because my voice hasn't got that tone. I would sound like a crooner singing hard rock.

At fourteen, I had another revelation. I was walking through a shopping mall with a friend. We spotted a cute girl, so my friend walked up to her and told her I thought she was cute. And then he said, 'Michael, sing for her.' So I sang. And I got her number and we dated. She was one of the first really cute girls I dated. And I got her through singing. It really hit me that there's power in that style of singing.

I had a rich fantasy life at this time, too. Every time I heard a song on the radio I fantasized it was me singing it. I'd sing into the mirror, pretending I was playing to a rapturous crowd at Madison Square Garden in New York. I'd watch a movie and fantasize that I was playing the lead role. There was always fantasizing and make-believe. As a teenager, I spent six summers working on my dad's salmon fishing boat. I'd sit there in the middle of the night on a four-hour wheel shift, listening to Tony Bennett, singing along and pretending I was singing with him. I wrote songs in my head while working on that boat.

My dad's boat was also the place where I learned to act like a man, not a bratty kid. My dad Lewis taught me that if I acted honourably with people, they would act honourably with me. His crew respected him, and that stuck with me. It was hard work, and we couldn't wear gloves because they'd get caught in the nets and rip our arms off. We put petroleum jelly on our hands while we slept to keep them from cracking and bleeding. At the end of a gruelling shift, my dad would take out a bottle of whisky and draw the halfway mark with a felt pen. He'd say, 'You can drink that much, boys, but no more.' And they'd respectfully drink to the line. He didn't want a bunch of hung-over guys working for him the next day. But, more importantly, he knew how to manage people without costing them their dignity. Those lessons have stuck with me to this day, especially now that I manage a staff of around a hundred people.

My dad taught me to work hard, so I began doing that at an early age. I started my career by playing any gig offered to me, as many as I possibly could. Nothing was too small. And, of course, I'd play for free, just to have an audience. I'd play to a construction crew during their coffee break if they'd take me. The audiences might not have paid much attention to this baby-faced kid in an ill-fitting suit his grandpa had given him, but I persevered and did my best to win them over. You'd think that a kid with that kind of ambition would be brimming with confidence, but I always suffered with that stage fright.

One time my grandpa heard about a talent show being held at the Big Bamboo, a popular nightclub in Vancouver. 'You should enter,' he told me, so I did, using a fake identification card, because I was a little under the legal drinking age of nineteen and wouldn't have been allowed inside a nightclub. My grandpa helped me practise 'It Had To Be You', over and over, and then we went down to the club. When my turn came, I sang my little heart out.

But I also made a total nuisance of myself to the poor woman who was organizing the show, a no-nonsense lady named Beverly Delich. She told me to shut up at least a couple of times. I had it coming. I mean, I was so excited I couldn't sit still. I kept saying, 'Is it my turn? Is it my turn?' And she said, 'Shut up and sit down.' She was really tough with me. I ended up winning the thing and, of course, I thought I'd made it. 'This is it. My first step to fame,' I said to my naïve young self.

The next morning, I had a phone call from Beverly. She said, 'Michael, the good news is, you're hugely talented. The bad news is, you lied about your age and you're disqualified from the competition.' I was so bloody mad I could barely contain myself. But Beverly went on to say that, although I'd lied about my age, she wasn't going to give up on me. And she didn't. I heard from her again.

born to sing

She had another competition for me to enter, specifically for talented youth between thirteen and twenty-one, at an annual fair that's hugely popular in Vancouver, the Pacific National Exhibition. I was seriously ticked off about losing my prize in the previous contest, and wasn't ready to listen to any of that, so I just said, 'Whatever. Goodbye.' But Beverly called back and talked with my parents. She told them, 'Your kid is too good not to do this talent contest at the PNE.'

That clinched it. My parents thought I should listen to her, so I did. She introduced me to Ray Carroll, a former member of the 1950s vocal group, the Platters. Ray taught me techniques to manage my stage fright, and other things, like how to hold a microphone properly, how to work with the band, how to do intros, how to get in and out, how to talk with the band while on stage, how to count tempos, all those little things that I had no clue about.

The PNE is located on the east side of Vancouver, and it's in operation from late summer to early September. It was there, among the rides, the shouting carnies, the prize-winning games, the cotton candy and the dog shows, that I won the Youth Talent Search that summer. It was 1995, and I was twenty years old.

It boosted my confidence tenfold. It made me think that I could have a crack at a professional singing career. I believed I was on my way, and I hadn't lied about my age, so the prize was mine.

To top it off, that night I landed my biggest paying gig, at a jazz club called Rossini's, for around fifty dollars. That was big-time money. Up until then, I'd been getting paid around twenty dollars a performance.

The PNE Youth Talent Search winner got to go to Memphis, Tennessee, to tour Elvis Presley's Graceland estate, and to compete in another talent contest, the International Youth Talent Search. Beverly would go with me. On the plane, I asked her if she would be my manager. Of course, because I was this brilliant young man, I put it to her like this: 'You know, Bev, I'm going to be huge here, this is my start. Would you want to be my manager?'

She turned her head and looked at me straight on. 'No,' she answered.

I said, 'But, Bev, I'll give you fifteen per cent of my earnings.'

And she said, 'Honey, what is fifteen per cent of nothing?'

I couldn't argue.

I went to Memphis and performed badly to a crowd of about two thousand people. I came third or fourth – and I was a terrible loser. I was the most ungracious person on stage. When they handed out the award they gave us all these silver plates. In front of everyone, I bent mine. When I went backstage, I kicked over tables, I threw stuff, I went nuts. The kid in me with the bad attitude emerged. I'm so embarrassed to think about what a jerk I was. We flew home.

Later, I called up Bev and had a heart-to-heart. I tried again to convince her to be my manager. I said, 'Bev, you can't quit on me if we're going to do this. You've got to promise me you'll never leave me.'

She said she'd do it. She had faith in me.

Suddenly, I had a manager. All I needed next was a career.

in
limbo
in
l.a.

Over the next couple of years, with Bev's help, I began playing around town, landing regular gigs and building a little following. Once I got the regular gigs, I knew how great it could feel to play for a crowd that was there for you, instead of a crowd that was there just to drink. Less than a year after my PNE win, we booked a gig in the bar at one of Vancouver's fancy old hotels, the Georgia Hotel downtown. I'd play to packed audiences every Saturday night for about eighty dollars. There were big windows that looked on to the street, and passers-by could see me playing with my band — local musicians Bev had helped bring together.

I'd sing classic tunes by Frank Sinatra, Dean Martin, Tony Bennett, and anything that would lend itself to swing, including my jazzy rendition of the *Spider-Man* theme song. I'd always loved it, and it was no accident that when I landed a major-label deal many years later, I immediately wanted to record it.

My timing was fortunate. There had been a big swing-music trend a couple of years earlier that was bolstered by the popularity of the 1996 Vince Vaughn movie, *Swingers*. Young audiences were already acclimatized to swing music and lounge-era jazz tunes, like 'Mack The Knife' and 'Summerwind'. As a consequence, there were other young swing acts in town, although most didn't follow the genre as purely as I chose to. I was a straight-ahead lounge act, nothing trendy or edgy about me, other than that I was twenty-one years old and attempting to charm my audiences. One of my earliest newspaper items read: 'He sounds like Harry Connick Jr and resembles Jason Priestley. At 21, Michael Bublé's dream is to perform at Madison Square Garden . . . For now, he'll have to content himself with packing them in at the Georgia Street Bar and Grill and living at home with Mom and Dad.' That blurb would prove prophetic.

I continued to play everywhere for any amount. One time, I played to about two thousand people with a well-known old-time Vancouver act that has been around for seventy years, the Dal Richards Orchestra. Bandleader Dal, who's in his nineties, is still going strong today.

In 1996, I landed a gig playing a private post-show backstage party for the Three Tenors on New Year's Eve. They were playing to fifty thousand people. My job was to entertain the tenors while they dined with their families. Nobody could have guessed that, one day, the night's dinner entertainment would be playing to crowds as big as a Three Tenors' audience.

I remember I was booked to play for about twenty minutes and one of the tenors' assistants came over and said they were enjoying what I was doing and I was to continue. He didn't say it in a nice way. I wasn't asked. It was an order. However, they paid me more because the gig went on longer.

Luciano Pavarotti, Placido Domingo and José Carreras looked like something in a zoo: they were behind these red ropes eating dinner with their families and people were taking pictures of them.

Just a year later, in the spring of 1997, I played to a sold-out audience at the Michael J. Fox Theatre in Burnaby, which holds about six hundred. It seemed like the entire Italian community had turned out, probably because my grandpa had invited them all. I even had groupies hanging around the front of the stage. It was a total kick. My friend Jack Cullen was in the crowd. He was a legendary old-time radio personality and played my songs on a popular local radio music show called *The Owl Prowl*. It was my very first radio exposure, and I'll never forget the thrill of hearing myself coming over the airwaves. It was like a drug.

That summer, a nightclub owner named Vance Campbell gave me a regular gig at a new, Havana-themed supper club called BaBalu. As soon as I performed for him, Vance became a huge supporter. It was a Sunday-night show hosted by a local radio DJ named Jason Manning, who was my age. He and I became fast friends. Manning had an AM radio show that played old jazz classics, including songs off my independently released CD, *First Dance,* on which I covered songs like 'I'll Be Seeing You' and 'All Of Me'. I am a total baby-face in the black-and-white close-up shot on the CD cover. I was just a kid. And I was so stoked to be getting radio exposure – even though, looking back, I imagine the number of listeners was minuscule. In those days, I was grateful if even one person bought my CD, which we were selling out of the trunk of my car. I was a hungry, eager kid.

I also played Monday nights at BaBalu, but it was on Sunday nights that my parents and Bev would come out and sit in the front row. The show quickly became a major draw, and I was pulling in around fourteen hundred dollars a night, which was a lot of money at the time. Of course, I had to pay my band out of it, so it didn't go far.

I also became the 'go to' guy for a national TV talk show called *The Vicki Gabereau Show.* Whenever they had a guest cancel, they'd call me as a replacement and I'd get into my suit and run down to the studio just for the chance to appear on TV. It was at one of these last-second fill-ins that I got to meet jazz singer Diana Krall, who's also from British Columbia.

Around this time I started doing some musical theatre and making better money. I co-starred in a musical called *Red Rock Diner,* in which I played a young Elvis Presley. It was during this production that I met my long-time girlfriend, the dancer, singer and actress Debbie Timuss. Debbie and I co-starred in another period musical, *Forever Swing,* in 1998. In both shows I got to pull out my favourite Elvis Presley moves, which I do to this day. I even had the honour of demonstrating them for Elvis's ex-wife, Priscilla Presley, backstage at my Los Angeles show in 2010. She was a very sweet and gracious lady, and she didn't laugh once.

Although I'd garnered some success as a local singer, my promising career felt like it was foundering. Nobody outside downtown Vancouver would have known my name, and even then I was known only to theatre-goers and lovers of lounge music. I was getting impatient to take it to the next level, but I wasn't sure how.

Forever Swing producer Jeffrey Latimer decided to take the show to Toronto, so Debbie and I went with it. In Toronto, I made decent money doing the musical, but it only lasted a couple of months. Afterwards I picked up some work playing regularly at the local clubs. Mostly, though, I found my career hitting another dead end. I began thinking about a career in broadcast journalism. I liked talking to people, and I had a flair for being on camera. Maybe I could make it work.

Beverly, however, thought I was being ridiculous. She said, 'Honey, you're too good. It's going to happen, I promise you. It's impossible for it not to happen. People are going to see you, and they will flock to you.' She believed in me, even when I was filled with self-doubt. For the first time in my life I really did wonder if I was deluded. It was an extremely dark period, that's for sure. I took a look around at all the other hungry actors and singers out there who'd never had a chance. Was I one of them? At the back of my mind a little voice was saying, 'It's never going to happen, Michael. You might have missed your chance already. You're going to be a poor nobody.' I was twenty-four or -five. Today, I think, How silly for a twenty-five-year-old to be feeling washed up. But at that age you don't feel like a kid. You're an adult, and you have to figure out a real way to make a living. Mommy and Daddy can't take care of you. You have to pay your bills and eat.

In those early years I released a couple more independent CDs, including *BaBalu* in 2001, and *Dream* in 2002. On *BaBalu*, I recorded the *Spider-Man* theme song, which would later be used in the 2004 Sam Raimi movie *Spider-Man 2* and also remixed by Junkie XL. I hear those self-made CDs of mine sell pretty well now on eBay. To think that back then I couldn't give most of them away. Also, I got nominated for a Canadian Genie Award for a song for an Eric McCormack movie, called *Here's to Life*. Eric is best known as the lead actor in TV's hit comedy *Will & Grace*. He's a fellow Canadian, and someone I now consider a friend.

By 2000, I'd done some TV and film, including a small role in a comedy-drama called *Duets*, starring Gwyneth Paltrow, directed by her dad Bruce Paltrow. That was about the most exciting thing that happened in my life at this time. Otherwise my career was in a holding pattern and I was seriously depressed.

And then a funny thing happened.

I got a break.

My bank account was almost drained when Jeffrey Latimer called me about a corporate event he was doing. He wanted to hire everybody who'd been in *Forever Swing*. It was good money, maybe three thousand dollars. I figured I could use it to pay my last rent cheque and buy a plane ticket home to Vancouver. I planned to call it quits. Enough was enough. It was time for me to get a proper job.

At the corporate gig, I met this guy named Michael McSweeney, who was assistant to former Canadian Prime Minister Brian Mulroney. Like I said, I'd play any gig at this juncture in my life, including weddings. Michael suggested I sing at the wedding of Brian Mulroney's daughter Caroline. I gave him one of my CDs, which he passed along to the Mulroneys. I got the gig, which was great, but then I found out that producer David Foster was going to be in the crowd. That changed everything.

For the uninitiated, David is a giant among music producers. He's produced Whitney Houston, Céline Dion, Madonna, Barbra Streisand, Michael and Janet Jackson — some of the biggest-selling names in music. He also happens to be from the west coast of Canada, like me. It was like the stars were lining up, and I was so thrilled I waived my performance fee. I told the Mulroneys I would perform for free, and I think that made them realize how badly I wanted to succeed. They couldn't have been nicer people.

At the wedding, Brian Mulroney encouraged David to pay attention to my singing. I heard later that Foster had been reluctant to listen carefully to the likes of a lowly wedding singer, but he came around – especially when he saw what a big hit I was with the audience. David told me later that Mulroney had said to him, 'You're not going to believe this kid.' Meanwhile, David was thinking, This is the last thing I want to do at a wedding, see some singer. But, thankfully, he loved what he heard. I believe he used the word 'transfixed'.

I saw it as the break I so desperately needed. David couldn't make any promises, but he told me that if I was willing to move to Los Angeles, he'd introduce me to important people and help me to make connections. He might have come to regret those words, because I took him up on it immediately. I called Bev and said, 'We're going to LA.'

David put me up at his house in Los Angeles while I performed at parties that he lined up – Bev travelled back and forth between Vancouver and LA. He was inducting me into his Hollywood world. He was good to me. He'd have dinner parties with famous people so I could meet them, and he'd take me along to parties and events that might help me further my career. I played private parties and charity events for audiences with faces as famous and varied as Mel Gibson, Sylvester Stallone, Muhammad Ali, Alice Cooper and Olivia Newton-John. The idea was to generate buzz throughout the industry and get people talking. I was terrified the whole time I performed for these people, but I was so desperate for a break that I pushed myself every step of the way. After I'd performed, I'd make a point of shaking everybody's hand and saying a few words of appreciation. I believe it's important to let people know who you are, to relate to them on a human level, no matter how famous or important they might be. At the end of the day, we all relate to each other as human beings, not as dollar signs or famous faces.

Back in Canada, I'd just spent seven years playing every wedding and dingy club in Vancouver and Toronto. Here I was, in Los Angeles, twenty-six years old, and so close to making the dream a reality that I could taste it. I wasn't about to settle into a career playing wedding parties for David's LA pals. I was hungry, and desperate for something to happen. In hindsight, I must have been an irritating pest, but what can I say? Sometimes you have to listen to that old adage about the squeaky wheel getting all the attention.

When I wasn't hounding David for a record deal, Bev was hounding him for me. David had made it painfully clear that he couldn't guarantee any kind of deal. In fact, he said at one point he'd never sign me. He said, 'You're great, I think you're marvellous, but I don't think that commercially I would know how to make it work. I don't think the company knows how to make this work. I will help you. You are on my radar. And if I can help you get gigs, or introduce you to people, I will do that.'

He lived up to his promise. He really did. He introduced me to just about everybody he knew. He coached me, counselled me, and became one of my closest friends. It's just that I still held out hope he could get me a record deal. I knew if I could get a deal, I could make records and people could finally hear me and decide for themselves if I was worthy. All of the celebrities who I'd played for liked me. Why wouldn't the public embrace me too?

David had told his friend Paul Anka all about me, and Paul expressed an interest in meeting the boy wonder who'd made an impression on the Hollywood party scene. I remember my first meeting with him. It was fall 2001, a week after 9/11. How could I forget the timing? David called me and asked me to play a benefit that comedian talk-show host Jay Leno was doing for Las Vegas casino workers who were hit hard in the aftermath of the atrocity because tourism was at an all-time low. We went to Vegas and I opened for Leno for two nights. I was so stoked that I partied till four or five a.m. when I finished the second night. I got absolutely wasted.

I had just gone to sleep when David woke me up with an early-morning phone call. He told me to get down to the MGM Grand Hotel to meet Paul Anka. I'll be honest: I was pretty hung-over and dazed, but Bev and I made our way to the MGM Grand, and we were soon seated in Paul's luxury suite, across from the legendary man himself. David was there too. Bev was almost vibrating, she was so nervous. She'd been a lifelong Paul Anka fan and here was her idol sitting in front of her, asking me to sing. With David at the piano, I sang Paul's mega-hit, which Frank Sinatra had made famous, 'My Way'. A couple of lines into the song, Paul said to David, 'This kid is great. Let's help him.'

And so began my friendship with Paul Anka. He said he'd help finance the record so that we'd have something to sell to a major label. David figured we needed about half a million dollars for the project. Around this time he tried to shape my image a bit. He suggested I change my name because he worried that they might call me 'Bubble'. But I pointed out that if someone with a clunky name like Christina Aguilera could have a successful career, surely 'Bublé' could stand up. He relented.

He also advised me to lose some of my baby fat. Hey, I'm Italian and I like my food. I especially like McDonald's burgers and I can eat several a day. I also like to cook. It's always been a challenge for me to turn down carbohydrate-laden food. I don't eat for sustenance, I eat because I love the taste of pepperoni pizza and a McDonald's Double Quarter Pounder with Cheese. I savour the food. For me, it's not about putting energy into my body, it's the enjoyment of eating. There's a reason that my name is now on the menu of a pizza joint in my hometown of Burnaby, BC.

Anyway, I started watching my diet and working out. David gave me other great advice. He told me to change my hair, ditch the cliché dinner jackets and polish my act. He wanted me to be more sophisticated, like a Brad Pitt-style movie star, not some schmaltzy lounge singer. He wanted me to be cool and suave, not the dork I really am.

I listened. I ate up every word that David told me. This guy is the winner of sixteen Grammys. He has written hit music and collaborated with Céline Dion, Barbra Streisand, Frank Sinatra, Michael Jackson, Chicago and Paul McCartney, and almost the entire mainstream radio roll-call of the 1980s and 1990s. He'd been in his own rock band in the 1970s, before focusing on songwriting and producing. He also kept a constant eye out for hot young talent. He'd just signed a young *protégé* named Josh Groban, the classical music/pop crossover, to his 143 Records imprint on Warner Bros Records, and Groban was taking off. That was what I wanted. I knew that David got his kicks helping mentor young, hungry talent. He wasn't in it for the money or fame any more. He liked the challenge of grooming talented junior singers for stardom. He told me he wasn't satisfied with his career so far in that department. By the time he'd worked with someone like Whitney Houston, for example, she'd already made a big name for herself. Same with Natalie Cole and Michael Jackson. He wanted to build careers from the ground up, and I wanted him to do that for me.

David was noncommittal – quite rightly. He knew it would be a challenge to get a deal for an artist who sang covers of the American songbook, especially when the recording industry was in a serious nosedive. People weren't buying records like they used to. And I don't make the kind of music that would sell through word-of-mouth downloads on the Internet. The music I make requires old-fashioned record-label marketing and distribution to reach my cross-generational audience.

I recorded some songs at David's Malibu recording studio, with David and producer-mixer Humberto Gatica, David's long-time friend and collaborator. Between the two of them, they've won more than thirty Grammys. They are giants in the business, so it's an understatement to say I was in good hands. We recorded 'Moondance', 'Kissing A Fool' and 'Fever'. They sounded great, and I was stoked. But I still didn't have a record deal. I needed to shop the demos around, show them off.

One night I was feeling particularly dejected that the demos might not go anywhere, that it was all for naught. Humberto told me to talk to David again, to really make my case for those recordings. It wasn't until I played yet another celebrity party — this one an anniversary event for Kenny G and his wife — that David decided to come through for me. Before the show, I pulled him aside and pleaded with him to go to Warner Bros and get me a shot at a record deal. I said, 'Please – I think what we do together could be magical. I think there's a void in the market. I think we can do this. Please take me – give me a shot . . . If they say no, I'll never bug you again. And if they just don't get it I won't bug you again. But these demos are magical.'

Of course, now I look back, I realize those demos are nothing like a full-on David Foster production. For budgetary reasons, they'd had to keep it simple. But to me, it was better than anything I'd heard before. He looked at me and I could see him processing it.

The next night he called me and said, 'Let's see what a twenty-six-year-old knows about the record business.' Those were his words exactly. Exactly. And he said, 'We're going to go to Warner Bros. I'm going to take you down. We're going to meet everybody. You're going to meet Tom Whalley.'

You know how they say, 'Be careful what you wish for'? Well, this was that moment for me. Finally I had pushed my way into a meeting with the top brass at Warner Bros Records, Tom Whalley. I was suddenly terrified. Meeting Tom Whalley turned out to be the best and worst day of my life. If I thought performing in front of celebrities was scary, I quickly discovered that performing in front of the chairman and CEO of Warner Bros Records was nothing short of a personal nightmare. My anxiety was through the roof. I was literally shaking. That tells you something about my nature. I may look comfortable onstage or on a television show, but I have fought long and hard with my own personal demons to get where I am – every step of the way. I am not a naturally brave person. I am, however, determined.

My nervousness must have been obvious to every executive sitting in the boardroom at Warner. Everyone was warm and friendly, and I'm sure they all felt for me. Here's the weird thing about the record industry when you're just starting out. They make you do awful things, like sing a cappella in a boardroom, under hideous fluorescent lights, to a group of office people who don't have a clue who you are and may not care. I had to perform for this group of sympathetic-looking executives who only knew they'd been pulled away from their work to see some cocky kid from Canada who thought he could be a singer. I was trying so hard to be myself, trying to look hungry without looking desperate. Afterwards, they said, 'Okay, Tom has five minutes to talk with you.'

It was like a scene out of a movie. I watched Tom Whalley walk down the hallway and he had a person on each side of him, barking orders and scheduling things. It was like *The Devil Wears Prada*, where Meryl Streep's character comes blowing in, surrounded by assistants. He sat down in his office and he had no expression on his face. He said, 'Hi, Bublé. Sit down.' And then he said, 'Why should I sign you? We have Sinatra on Reprise already.' Reprise under the Warner Bros Records umbrella: they own part of the Sinatra catalogue. He'd made his point.

Now it was my turn to make mine. I told him, 'With all due respect, Mr Whalley, Sinatra is gone. I'm sure he didn't want to have the music buried with him. There's a void in the market and there's room for me. I'll kill for you. I'll work my ass off. Listen to these demos. I'm not telling you I know anything about the record business, I just know this could be big. We could make this massive.'

And he gave me no reaction, nothing discernible. I have no clue what he thought of me, if he believed me, whether he really liked the demos he heard or not. He only told me he understood this kind of music.

I walked out thinking I'd just seen my chance come and go. I didn't feel bad – just numb, terrified, nervous, scared, exhilarated.

I don't think David knew what had happened, either. He had just had success with Josh Groban at Warner, which gave him leverage to make the case for another young male singer. But when you sign an act, you throw almost a million dollars out of the window right there. It's a really big risk. David stuck his neck out for me.

No matter what happens in my life, what David says to me, or if we get into an argument, I will always be loyal to him. I will never forget what he did for me. I will never forget the way that he put himself in a precarious position, business-wise, for me.

You want to know how anxious I was after that meeting? I called my grandpa Mitch and asked him to fly down to LA and stay with me. So he did. He flew down to hold my hand through one of the most stressful times in my life, while I waited to see what Mr Whalley had in store for me. There I stood, at that moment in life when it all comes down to a phone call. And it would be a phone call like no other.

An agonizing six days later, I was on the treadmill in the basement gym at my apartment building. The doors opened. My grandpa walked in with Bev right behind him. Both of them were crying. They told me to call David right away. He had good news.

I was shaking. Just shaking. Every bit of my heart was in my gut. I picked up the phone and called him, and he said, 'Hey, Mike, hey, man. I want you to feel safe because you have a great family and I want to welcome you to Warner. Congratulations on being my new act. We love you. And your journey is just beginning. Welcome.'

That was it. It was 2002, I was twenty-six years old, and after ten years of playing weddings and dives, I had a record deal. I thought my heart was going to beat right out of my chest. I was to be signed with David's 143 Records label, which is part of Reprise. We wouldn't need Paul to find us investors, after all.

It was time to make a record. David assembled a bunch of session players, including a rhythm section and four horns. With my money from the record deal, I rented a luxury apartment in a posh neighbourhood called Westwood. I didn't

in limbo in l.a.

have a lot of money, so I slept on an air mattress and used a cardboard box for a table. Bev continued to fly back and forth between LA and Vancouver.

I spent my days at David's recording studio in Malibu. With David and Humberto at my side, I spent five months recording classics like 'Come Fly With Me', 'For Once In My Life', 'The Way You Look Tonight', 'You'll Never Know', 'All of Me', as well as David's recommendations – George Michael's 'Kissing A Fool', the Bee Gees' 'How Do You Mend A Broken Heart?' and Queen's 'Crazy Little Thing Called Love'. We also included Paul's classic, 'Put Your Head On My Shoulder'. Paul helped with the song selection and guided me as an artist. David was there for the daily grind of the recordings.

David was tough on me in a good way. He pushed me to deliver. Paul was also really good to me in a tough-love sort of way. Those guys had decades of experience in the music business. They were self-made success stories and they'd won tons of awards and accolades. I have tremendous respect for them and I soaked up everything they taught me. In those early days, I was like a puppy looking for training.

Bev realized that she couldn't manage me on her own: we needed to find either a co-manager or someone with more experience to take over. David called his former manager Bruce Allen, who's based in Vancouver and responsible for building the careers of legendary rock acts Bryan Adams, Loverboy, Bachman Turner Overdrive and country star Martina McBride. He had also revitalized the career of Canadian superstar Anne Murray. Bruce has become a legend in the industry. He's a well-known workaholic, who represents his clients with the intensity of an angry pit bull. He's also a music aficionado and hardcore Elvis Presley fan. I wanted him for my manager. Besides, we hit it off. Bev knew that Bruce had the connections and experience to see me through to the next stage of my career. From Bruce's perspective, I had Warner Bros Records backing me, which would make his job easier.

Of course, Bev stayed on until I made the transition to Bruce's management team. It was an emotional time. Everybody on my new team adored Bev, including publicist Liz Rosenberg, who works with Madonna. She came on board and is with me to this day. As for Bev, she'll always be the key person who launched my career, as well as a dear friend who's more like a member of my family. She gave up a big chunk of her life for me, and I will always be grateful to her.

I've been lucky that the people around me have proven to be so intensely loyal and hardworking. Bruce cares about the longevity of my career. He's not in the record business: he's in the career business. He has a personal attachment, a belief. Even when we're having our usual arguments, I always know that if I was fighting a war, there is no one I'd rather have beside me than Bruce. In this business, you need a manager like that.

When our record was finished, we played it in David's office at Warner Bros. My grandpa was there, of course, and he said, 'Gee, what do you think? Can we sell twenty or thirty copies?'

David said, 'Grandpa, if this kid doesn't do fifty to a hundred thousand copies, you ain't going to see another record.'

I came crashing right back down to reality. As an independent singer, it had taken me a decade to sell 10,000 to 15,000 records of my own, out of cars and at tables at the back of clubs. How was I going to sell 100,000?

taking
control

The first album was self-titled and it was released on 11 February 2003, strategically timed for Valentine's Day. I remember doing press for it beforehand, and being really nervous. David and Paul got involved in the interviews to help promote it. Paul told my hometown newspaper, 'It's important that I help him, and it'll go down that I helped this guy be a big star . . . When you have that kind of voice, you could ultimately sing the phone book.'

David told the same reporter, 'He could have a thirty-year career. I don't know if you could say that about every rock act that's out there right now.'

Bev weighed in too: 'Maybe I didn't have all the connections, but I always worked my ass off for him. And I believed in him. I never stopped believing.'

On the outside, I tried to look confident, but inside I was worried. Would I make them proud? Would I go down in history as another record-label success story or a soon-to-be-forgotten failure? I suddenly felt I had a lot to prove – to my family, my girlfriend, my friends, my producers, my manager and my record label. It was my moment of truth, as if the world was challenging me: 'Okay, Bublé, you wanted a shot at the big-time. Now show us what you got.'

Nobody could believe the reaction to the record. Within weeks, it was climbing the charts. Suddenly the 50,000 in sales we were praying for seemed paltry. To our amazement, it had soon sold two million copies worldwide. Clearly, we were on to something.

At the time, David and I liked to tell people that all the little pieces of the puzzle were coming together, and they truly were. I was a multi-platinum-selling international artist. I still had so much more to prove — but, hey, I finally had their attention. That first album went platinum in the UK and Canada, reaching the top ten on the albums charts. It went to number one on the Australian chart. By 2004, it was on Billboard's top 200. Singles 'Kissing A Fool', 'How Can You Mend A Broken Heart?' and 'Sway' reached the top thirty of the adult contemporary chart.

Goofy headlines started popping up, stuff like 'He's got the world on a string.' I found myself singing 'I'm Dreaming Of A White Christmas' on CNN's hugely popular *Larry King Live*. David and I did a Christmas EP that year, called *Let It Snow*. It was a brilliant way to get me television exposure around the holidays. I also picked up a few small acting parts around this time, with a small role in the movie *The Snow Walker*, and a couple of parts on TV. Although music is my passion, all forms of entertainment fascinate me. I remember taking tons of theatre classes as a kid and going to Tuesday movie nights at the local cinemas.

Also in 2004, I won the Best New Artist award at Canada's biggest music awards, the Junos. The album was nominated for Album of the Year, but it lost to Sam Roberts. It hardly mattered. Other pieces were falling into place. By this time we'd auditioned for a touring band, starting with the crucial role of musical director. I knew I'd be spending a lot of time with the MD, so I was fussy. We held an audition in Los Angeles, and Bruce's long-time associate Randy Berswick, David and David's sister Jaymes all sat in on it. In my mind, I had already settled on a wonderful, mature, extremely intelligent piano player who'd already auditioned. But then in walked Alan Chang, this tall, handsome Asian-American guy who could play piano equally well. I have to admit, I initially held his looks and youth against him. David, Randy and Jaymes were keen on him. I wasn't.

The conversation went something like this.

'This is the kid you need. See how good-looking he is. And he plays so well.'

'What are you talking about?' I shot back. 'What the hell is this? The Backstreet Boys? I need a musical director. I know how difficult that position is, and how important it is, and it has to be filled by someone who really has the maturity to do it.'

As with most arguments at this early stage, I relented. It turned out that they were right. Alan wasn't just a pretty face, but one of the best writers, arrangers and producers I could have hoped for. He co-writes my songs with me, travels on my tour bus, and he has turned into one of my best friends. He's the perfect guy to take on the road because he's so even-tempered. I like to have fun on the road, so I prefer having guys like Alan on the bus with me so we can chat, listen to music and play video games, post-show. It's important that there's a good rapport and camaraderie there. We put together a band comprising a rhythm section and four horns, and of that early touring band, Alan and two other guys are still with me today.

If I hadn't hired Alan as my musical director, I'd have made a bad call. I may be wilful, but I am also my father's son, and my father taught me one of the most essential skills that a businessman or entrepreneur can possess: to surround yourself with honest, loyal and skilled people, and to know when to bow to their expertise. A huge part of success is the ability to know your strengths *and* your limitations. At that stage in my career, I might have still been feeling my way, but the years I'd spent on my dad's fishing boat had equipped me with respect for those more experienced than I am.

The boat was around eighty feet long, and had a crew of five guys. I started working on it in the summer when I was thirteen years old. I was unsure and quiet, humbled by my dad's sometimes rough-talking men. By the time I was sixteen, I knew exactly what I was doing on that boat, and I'd become a pretty good skiff man. It was a purse seiner with a drum on the back, which is like a big spool of thread but with a net on it that can scoop up entire schools of fish. I would take the skiff maybe fifty feet from the boat to the beach, throw an anchor over and tie the net off to a tree or rock so that we could tow the line away from shore. It was an important job with a lot of responsibility, and I was good at it. It was a lot of fun, too, but most importantly, it taught me how to behave with adults, and to respect them. At school, we behaved like a bunch of bullies. But when you're on a boat with hard-working men, you learn a thing or two about common respect. I was an immature kid, but every time I returned to school after one of those summers on the boat, I was more aware of other people's feelings, and knew that when you show you respect, you receive it.

Those summers on the boat helped shape me into the man I am today, but that's not to say my lessons weren't learned the hard way. When I was sixteen, feeling cocky about my skiff-man skills and the fact that I was the son of the boss, I decided to play boss man with this crew guy named Stubbs. He was around six foot five and weighed 220 pounds, a twenty-four-year-old street kid from suburban Ontario who was a super-easygoing but tough guy. I was crew chief because I'd been there longer than any of the other guys at that time. When the net got damaged, it had to be fixed right away with netting needles, which had to be kept filled and ready to go. My dad had told me to tell Stubbs to fill the needles, but instead of asking him nicely I made it an order. I went down into the fo'c'sle, which is the forward section of the boat, and I said, 'Stubbs, you gotta go fill up the needles.'

He said, 'What?'

I said, 'Go fill up the goddamn needles.'

He said, 'Don't talk to me like that.'

I said, 'Listen, if I tell you to jump, you ask me how high.'

He looked at me. And then – whack! He head-butted me so hard, he knocked me out. When I came to seconds later, he said, 'I don't give a f**** who you or your daddy is. No one ever talks to me like that, you piece of shit. And you can go run to your daddy and tell him what I did.'

I was so embarrassed by my behaviour that I never mentioned the incident to my father or anyone else until much, much later. I don't know why I acted the way I did, other than that I simply wasn't happy with myself in those early years. I was riddled with self-doubt, and I had to learn the hard way that putting other people down wasn't going to make me superior. Suffice it to say, I never, ever talked to anyone that way again.

The lessons on that fishing boat stuck with me. And so, many years later, when in the company of my more experienced elders, I knew I had to let them lead, and I showed them respect — even when deep inside I was eager to be the boss.

Bruce started me off with an appearance on NBC's *Today* show for Valentine's Day. A couple of days later, I did a showcase to about forty people in New York, then went to Los Angeles and played for two weeks at the Roosevelt Hotel in the Cinegrill room, with Alan and my new band. The New York show was a technical disaster, but I managed to do damage control and win the crowd over. As for the shows at the Roosevelt, they started generating a lot of buzz and became a bit of a scene, selling out every night. David brought famous friends to these events, while record-label executives and agents came out to hear the new kid.

I felt comfortable and confident moving among the crowd, chatting with everybody and casually introducing a few of my songs. By 2004, I had a major booking agent and was on the road, playing 1,000-capacity theatres in the US, Milan, Hamburg and Paris. Bruce brought in his long-time promoter friend Don Fox to handle the US shows, and Don is still a major part of my career today. I also met Australian promoter Paul Dainty around this time, and he still handles my shows in Australia.

By the time my first record got to the two million mark, David and Bruce realized that I was on to something and they should start letting me take charge of my career. They could see that I was marketable, not just because I could sing but because I knew how to entertain people.

For my second album, 2005's *It's Time*, I wanted to put my own artistic stamp on it instead of merely following everybody's advice. I felt I had earned the right to do that.

On the first record, I'd tried fighting to get my own way but, let's face it, I was a junior surrounded by veterans. I lost every argument, quite rightly. I understand it. If I'd been in their shoes, trying to help a totally unproven kid who didn't know anything about the business, I'd have shot down my ideas too. I mean, who knows more about choosing songs than a guy like Paul Anka? I bowed to their experience.

But with the second record, I won a few more arguments. Even David conceded that he had to listen to me now.

Later, when it was finished, I asked David if I had messed things up for him because I was so involved. He said, 'Yeah, you did. It's harder now because you step on my toes more and more, and I know I have to give you more respect and power,' which was a very honest thing for him to say. He said it tongue-in-cheek, though, and I know he's pretty proud of me. I remember I called him after my hit single 'Home' was released and told him about all the radio stations in the US that were adding it to their playlists. I was bouncing off the ceiling. I had written a hit song, which felt amazing. He joked, 'You're going to phase me out. You won't need me any more. You go and write a song and it's a huge hit.'

I said, 'Get out of here,' because I couldn't have done any of it without him. David is one of my best buddies to this day. We may argue a lot in the studio, but neither of us takes it home with us. We have a lot of fun working together and hanging out. One time a Canadian reporter came down to LA to do a story on me and spend time watching me record. He was a super-cool guy, also named David. He said he hadn't expected it to be so much fun, and he asked if he could stay in the studio another day. He said, 'I have something to tell you. I actually have everything I need for the story. I just feel like hanging out with you guys for a while longer.' He ended up staying three more days.

I didn't have it all my own way on the second album, however. There was one exception, and that was the Sinatra cover, 'I've Got You Under My Skin'. I didn't want to do such a straight-ahead classic because I didn't want to get the usual criticism of being a tribute artist. That is one of the most identifiable Sinatra songs in his repertoire. As much as I love the song, I really feared being seen as a tribute artist. Remember, I wasn't as confident as I am now. I hadn't fully developed my own identity. But Bruce and David were adamant. David said, 'You've got to get this song on the record.'

I said, 'No. I've made it my record from start to finish. It's representative of me, and these are my songs, my arrangements, and I put my treatment all over it. Unlike the first one, I've grown. You can hear the maturity.'

David and Bruce said something like, 'Michael, two million people bought that record and they bought it because you brought them comfort. "I've Got You Under My Skin" might be one of the greatest arrangements ever written.' And they said, 'People expect a certain thing from you now. You can't just go off in another direction after all these people have invested in you.' I gave in. Maybe they were right. After all, they'd been right so far.

I sang it like it was my own song. I tried to make it mine. I don't sing like Sinatra, anyway. I sing on my vowels, which was how my vocal coach taught me, and it's the way I like to sing. I always enunciate my vowels. Not everybody does that.

It's a strange thing. Some artists of my generation who also cover the American songbook often make a point of distancing themselves from this kind of music. They'll try to modernize the songs, or use gimmicks, or put their stamp all over it to the point at which the original is unrecognizable. I've always been of the mind that I want to respect the singers who came before me. I want to put my own stamp on the classics, but I also want to keep them alive. Frank is gone, Bobby Darin is gone, as are Dean Martin and others. I feel duty-bound to honour their music instead of trying to distance myself from it.

I'm not the next Sinatra. There will never be another Sinatra, but I do want people to know all over the world that there is a guy who will continue to do this for them, who will keep the songs alive, carry on the legacy of those singers, because almost everyone else has run away from it.

I don't know why people are so afraid to embrace it. I've said to many critics and writers, 'Would you rather bury Frank?' They can't seem to get over the fact that somebody born in 1975 might understand his music, and might be passionate about it, and might do it well.

These days, I'm not worried about being viewed as a Sinatra clone, or anything like that. I think I've been around too long now for that to be the perception, and people know better. I have my own style, but I don't go out of my way to distance myself too much from anybody else. That's not my concern, maybe because I'm also a songwriter. These last few years I've more than proven that I'm not a tribute act. I've done the songs my own way, I've done the shows my own way, and it's worked. I believe we're coming up with a new style of music. It's so simple, kind of a hybrid of traditional pop and standards, or popular jazz – whatever you want to call it.

I took some serious risks with the second record, too. I included the Beatles song, 'Can't Buy Me Love'. You might not think it's a big risk to include a song by one of the biggest pop acts in history, but that's precisely why it is such a risk. I had to wrestle with the idea because the critics could skewer a so-called crooner for having the audacity even to think he could go near Beatles territory. But I approached the terrific Grammy-winning arranger John Clayton with the idea, and he and I came up with a jazzy rendition that perfectly captured my style and honoured the Beatles classic at the same time. I loved it.

I said, 'John, I want you to come up with a smoking version of this song. I want it to be Michael Bublé's version.' I had made a very conscious decision to include it. I'd thought it through carefully. Do I make a record for the critics or do I make a record for the people? Could I handle waking up in the morning and seeing critics slagging me every day? Yes, I could.

My biggest critic and adviser is my mom. She'll always tell me the truth.

I called her and played the Beatles song for her. 'What do you think?' I asked.

She said, 'I hate it.'

I said, 'What's your favourite song?' She said her favourite song of mine was 'Save The Last Dance.' She loves the energy of it.

I've noticed that if you're under forty years old, you like my Beatles cover. If you're over forty, you probably don't. Older people say, 'Don't mess with the Beatles. They're iconic!' The same thing happened when I did 'Moondance' on the first album. Bruce called and said, 'Get it off the record.' Not just him, but everyone at the label.

I said, 'No.'

He said, 'The critics are going to kill you. You can't touch Van Morrison. He's done the definitive version.'

But I said, 'No. If I make it mine, then it becomes my song.' And look what happened. My version of 'Moondance' became a hit.

On the second album, I also brought in legendary producer Tommy LiPuma on the Harry Warren song 'The More I See You'. Tommy had produced Miles Davis, Natalie Cole, Barbra Streisand and Diana Krall, just to name a few. We worked on the song with producer and engineer Al Schmitt. Tommy and Al have won dozens of Grammys.

Another idea I had for the album was to do a duet with Canadian superstar Nelly Furtado. Nelly had achieved stardom with her 2000 major-label début and her mega-hit 'I'm Like A Bird'. I loved her voice, and I thought she would lend the perfect seductive tone to an Italian pop song from the 1960s 'Quando Quando Quando'. I loved the idea of having her on that song so much that if she couldn't do it I was going to nix the song from the album. But I didn't want to ask her myself because that would put her on the spot. I got Bruce to check with her manager and she immediately said yes. She came into the studio and I already knew she had a lovely voice, but I was struck by its power. I kept telling her how amazing she was, and she was so humble and sweet. And she really got into the song. She totally dug it and thought it was really romantic. It spoke to her. The result was super-sexy. Nelly killed it. She even did a version in her ancestral Portuguese, just to have for herself.

I love Otis Redding, but I hadn't ever really listened to the words to his hit 'Try A Little Tenderness' until I was sitting in a jazz club in Australia and heard this girl singing. She sang the words, 'She may be weary, and women do get weary . . . ' and I was mesmerized. It got me excited, and I started to come up with all these ideas about how to do the song. I thought it would be really cool to take 'Tenderness' and make it a beautiful ballad where every word is distinct, and you can feel the emotion of it. At the end, there's this Redding-type thing happening where it goes, 'You've got to squeeze her . . ./You've got to try and always please her . . . ' and it builds up. That's my favourite part. I wait for it.

Then there was the wonderful Nina Simone song 'Feeling Good'. When I brought it into the studio as a possibility for the record, David and Humberto said no. They didn't get it. They didn't think it would work. But I kept playing it through my iPod on the speakers and by the fifth day they had changed their minds. Suddenly they thought it was a great tune. Sometimes you have to listen to something a few times before you really hear it. I told them, 'We're three guys sitting here and we're making records for a heck of a lot of women. We need to have a sensitive side.'

My girlfriend at the time, Debbie, would be sitting there too, and we'd ask her what she thought. She would hear a song and most of them either made her cry or got her in the mood for love, if you know what I mean. It's so nice to have a female point of view in the studio. We surveyed a lot of other girlfriends, wives and women from the label or my manager's office. Their feedback was vital. And they all gave 'Feeling Good' the big thumbs-up. It turned out to be one of my most popular covers. The crowds go wild for it to this day.

It was with the second album that I really came into my own as a songwriter. I'd been messing around writing songs since I was a teenager on my dad's fishing boat. But humming a melody to yourself is very different from performing it in a studio with fellow musicians who throw in chords and lyrics and brainstorm with you about how to shape it. And to hear your own song on the radio is to feel like a true artist, somebody who has something to say to the world. It's one thing to be an interpretive artist, which I am, and proudly too, but I'll always need to write my own songs. I seem to have a knack for coming up with melodies, which has made the process flow quite naturally.

'Home' was the first single I'd ever written, and is still my biggest hit. The song was used in a Debra Messing movie called *The Wedding Date*, and it was the only original track on *It's Time*. I was in Italy and I was on tour, and I was feeling really good about my life. But I had been on the road for about seven months, and I hadn't seen Debbie in ages. One day I was in the shower and I started singing, 'Another summer day has come and gone away/In Paris and Rome/But I want to go home . . . ' It came really easily. I love pretty melodies, and the words to this song are so simple. Then I got to the point where I realized that it was becoming autobiographical. I got to the bridge and thought, I'm getting so close to this song, I'm having a hard time being objective. I called David's daughter Amy Foster, who's a songwriter. She has a really lively, upbeat personality and a razor sharp wit – she's a real Canadian. We'd written a bunch of songs together already and she's a great lyricist.

I said I needed a nice bridge that was honest. 'I feel that what I write is corny because I'm writing about my own life. I don't feel bad for myself, I don't pity myself, but I need it to come across that I'm a guy who misses home. I miss the love of my life.' Amy came up with some great lyrics, just little things that made the difference for me, stuff like, 'I feel just like I'm living someone else's life/ that I just stepped outside'. Then I added, 'And I know just why you couldn't come along/ This was not your dream ...' and she wrote a line that really helped me: 'Another aeroplane/another sunny place/I'm lucky I know/ and I want to go home.' She called me and insisted that we needed to say this, that it had to be my story, not some generic version.

When she sang it to me over the phone, I thought, God, that's what I wanted to say. That's perfect. I love it that she writes lyrics that aren't cliché.

My musical director Alan Chang punched out some of the chords for the song.

I had more original material I could have put on the record, but I didn't use it because I needed to keep the continuity of sound with the previous album. I wanted to grow as an artist, but I didn't want to alienate my new audience. 'Home' is a different-sounding song from the rest on the album. It's got a country twang to it.

When I make an artistic decision, I conduct a poll. I go around and ask people for their feedback. My management team will ask me, 'Why do you care?' I respond that I care more about what the average person thinks than some executive at a record company. It's the fans who buy the records. I want to know what they think.

After I wrote 'Home,' I brought the song with me into a Warner Bros Records meeting and said, 'Listen to this song I wrote.' I played it for them and they went ballistic. I'd thought 'Feeling Good' should be the first single, but they put out 'Home' instead. Jo Faloona, who used to work at my record label and is now on my management team, explained to me that if you have a strong song, then a handful of stations will add you every week. Our first day, we had eighteen stations add the song. The power of radio had opened doors for me. I was suddenly sitting with a number-one hit, and it was my first original song. Today, the album has sold six million copies, and it's all because of 'Home'.

The record label wanted a video for it, which I made in Vancouver at the beautiful old Orpheum Theatre. All of a sudden, the song was getting airplay all over the world. It still gets used as the soundtrack to sad stories about guys who've gone off to war and miss their families, that type of thing. I think we all relate to it because we all know what it's like to be homesick. It's one of the worst feelings. I know about that as well as anybody, because I'm only home for a few weeks a year.

For a good part of my life I'm either getting ready to go on stage, I'm on stage, or I'm winding down after being on stage. When I perform, I worry about my audiences. It matters a lot to me what they think, what they want. It always has, even in those early years. I've always liked to tease the men in my audience for wanting to be somewhere else, as if they were dragged along to a screening of the *Sex and the City* movie or something.

My fans know that I like to joke around. I regard myself as more of an entertainer than a singer, and not too many singers incorporate actual stand-up comedy into their set lists, but I'm comfortable doing it, and I really think it adds a lot to the show. People come and see me to feel good, to have fun. I'm not a navel-gazing singer-songwriter type who requires his audience to sit rapt and pay close attention. I want them dancing in the aisles, whooping it up, laughing, clapping, making out with their dates, if it moves them. The jokes are a natural fit.

I might be the most accessible artist around. I love interacting with the crowd, and at every show I get off my pedestal, which is the stage, and go right down into the audience to mingle with everybody. I love seeing the faces of my fans up close. I can't do it as much any more because of my crazy schedule, but I used to stand outside my bus and sign autographs for an hour. I'd have members of my crew telling me to get on the bus and I'd tell them to leave me alone. If I don't have time to sign autographs afterwards, I'll sign them during the show, or for an hour beforehand. I sign hundreds of CD covers to make them just a little more personal. I tell you, I still can't get over the fact that people pay to see me – and I probably never will.

It reminds me of a guy I met when I was starting out, a Canadian artist named Johnny Favourite. He was doing better than I was at the time, but he said, 'Kid, I'm telling you, you're the one. Wait till you experience the joy of going on stage when people have paid hard-earned money to see you. It will make it all so easy.' I never forgot what he said to me, and it turned out to be absolutely true.

One day, not long after *It's Time* was released, I was watching TV, and Tony Bennett was on a talk-show. The interviewer asked him if he had any opinion on the new singers out there. At first he said it would be unfair to say he had a favourite. Then he said, 'No. Michael Bublé is my favourite. He makes these songs his own. He can sing.'

Well, that comment just blew me away. It beat out anything that any critic could say about my music. This is a guy who's the real deal. You can't get more authentic than Tony Bennett. So for him to be telling people that they should embrace me, that I am the one carrying the torch – well, it doesn't get more thrilling than that. That's exactly how I want to be seen, what I want my legacy to be. I want to be the guy who carries the torch and makes his musical heroes proud. What better legacy could there be?

But I had to be my own man and take charge artistically if I was to make a go of this career thing. Also, I wanted to be responsible for my own album. If it went on to sell ten copies, I'd take the blame and say it was my own fault rather than blame somebody else. I needed to do the third record my way.

making
it
big

By the time I got to my third album, my life had become bigger, faster and a lot more complicated.

I was calling the shots, to some extent, but there was another exciting offshoot of my success around this time: I could afford to give my family the kind of presents that were life-changing – for example, I could help my sister financially so that she could stay at home with her children, which was a huge boost to her quality of life. I was really proud to make my success a part of their lives and legacy, not just my own.

But there was another side to fame, and it was a lot darker. I was going through a difficult adjustment period in my life. I had craved success, but I hadn't realized the impact of it.

Suddenly a lot of people seemed to be paying attention to me, and with that newfound fame came a lot of responsibility and adjustment.

During the making of the third album, I was doing a video for my single 'Everything'. I had been on set since four a.m., it was now around six p.m., and I was in my trailer sleeping because I had a fifteen-minute break before getting back to work. Bruce called and said that Tony Bennett was not well and he'd had to pull out of his *American Idol* performance. The show's producers wanted me to replace him. My first concern was that Tony was ill. When I found out he had a cold, my next concern became a serious case of stage fright. I was terrified.

I have spent a lot of my career being terrified. But I love my job so much and hunger for it so much that it overrides the terror. I have a friend who had to MC at a wedding. He called me and said he was so nervous he was having an anxiety attack. I said, 'Dude, that's my life.' It often happens to me. If I know I have to go on *American Idol* or some other live TV show, I get scared. I'm asking myself, 'Can I do it? What if I'm so nervous I pass out or throw up? What if I forget the words?' However, in my live concert shows, I'm backstage kicking a ball around, I'm so comfortable before I go on stage. There's a big difference between television and concert performance: the interaction I have with the audience. At a live show, if I forget the words, I can just joke with the audience and win them over so that they'll forgive me. On television, in front of fifty million faceless people, I don't have that luxury. You either nail it or blow it completely. I've seen entertainers really blow it on live programmes and I feel so badly for them because it hurts just to see it. It's for that reason that I won't sing national anthems at sports games.

When I get to interact with my audience from the stage and have actual conversations by jumping into the crowd, I'm a happy man. I'm in my comfort zone. I feel like one of them, like the brother, the boyfriend, the husband. I know how they're feeling and I can relate to them. I think of myself as a real guy's guy who somehow ended up wearing a suit and singing love ballads.

Also, if I screw up in a live TV performance I'll hear about it from my friends and family. My performance on *American Idol* was not one of my best. I was so nervous some people thought I was drunk. When I called my mother, she just said, 'You looked nervous.' I wish people could meet me and sit with me because they would quickly see that I'm not some croony boy who sings croony love songs: I'm not confident enough to be that. When I look in the mirror, I still see an insecure fourteen-year-old who's eager to please. Unlike Frank or Dean, or any of those boys who sang the songs before me, I'm anything but cool.

Let me give you an example. It was around this time that I was nominated for a Grammy for Best Traditional Pop Vocal Album for my live release *Caught In the Act*. I'd been nominated the year before for my second album *It's Time*, but I'd lost to Tony Bennett, who, as I've already established, is my idol. The category is untelevised, so the awards are presented in a separate ceremony. A Canadian reporter interviewed me, and asked me how I felt about the Grammy nomination. I commented that it was unfair that the category wasn't televised. Then, in good-natured ribbing to my competitor Tony, I jokingly said something like, 'Hey, Tony's going to win anyway, why would I go?'

I was referring to the fact that Tony had won more times than anyone else ever in the history of the category, and also, if anybody deserved to win again, it was Tony. To my horror, the reporter wrote it as if I'd made the comment seriously. It made me look like an ungrateful jerk, and I was horrified me to think that Tony might read it and think I was being disrespectful. The thought of unintentionally insulting him nearly destroyed me. I worry enough about unintentionally insensitive remarks I make to people I don't idolize. When I apologize to them days later, they don't even know what I'm talking about. You can imagine how I'd beat myself up about insulting my music hero. Tony and I have had many discussions, and I think he likes that I have a strong understanding and appreciation of the history of this music, this genre. I'm not just in it for the cheap thrill of nostalgia. I feel like a student with the master when I'm with Tony, and I see myself carrying on the tradition of the masters who came before me.

The night my comment went public, I lost a lot of sleep and, as a result, I became wary of speaking with the media. I had clearly made a sarcastic comment, which was my nature. If a reporter was going to take me literally when I did this, what hope did I have of surviving the fame game? I'm far too thin-skinned to be raked over the media coals in that way. I had my management issue the following statement: 'I'm extremely honoured to have been nominated for a Grammy in the Best Traditional Pop Vocal Album category. I did indeed make my feelings known that the category should be broadcast live during the award ceremony. This category honours the interpreters of some of the greatest songs ever written. There are millions of people like me who love and respect this music. I jokingly said that Tony Bennett is going to win anyway, so why should I go? This is not sour grapes. I worship, love and respect Tony Bennett. He is my idol. I voted for him and he deserves to win.'

That year Tony won the Grammy, and at the ceremony we had a nice chat. He told me to be careful, not to feel like I had to fight the battle on behalf of all the vocalists who felt the category should be televised. He mentioned that his friend Frank Sinatra had made a similar comment and paid the price of backlash for it. He asked me if I felt honoured to be nominated. I said, 'Of course!' And he told me that I should only ever talk about the honour I felt because anything else would sound ungrateful. Throughout my life, I've absorbed a lot of wisdom from older, more experienced guys. I took Tony's gentle advice the same way — I ate it up.

As it turned out, my third album, *Call Me Irresponsible*, would win the Grammy for Best Traditional Pop Vocal Album the next year. I simply said I was honoured.

When I began making *Call Me Irresponsible*, I decided I was ready to take full responsibility for calling the shots. I'd earned it. I wanted to include a couple of my own songs, and record live, in the studio, like in the old days of Sinatra. I was very proud of my first record, but it didn't feel like mine. David Foster and Humberto Gatica had had to make very simple choices with it because we had budget restrictions. They said, 'Let's just sell this record and get you out there. Then you can worry about your ego or your pride or your art.' That was totally fair. After all, I was new to the business. Who was I to start making demands?

making it big

With the second one, *It's Time*, I took a little more control. I started to put my foot down about certain things and made it more my own record.

By now I'd won five Juno Awards, which are Canada's version of the American Grammys and the UK's Brit Awards. I had a huge hit with 'Home' from the second album. I had gone from a one-truck tour to a five-truck tour with a thirteen-piece band.

On the third album, I wrote and released two more songs that would become hits, 'Lost' and 'Everything'. I was proving myself as a songwriter, even though a lot of people would continue to think I was only covering other people's songs. I remember I was on my dad's boat, in his cabin. We had double bunks. I was in the bottom one, writing down the words to a song: 'I miss the way that you walk/the way that you talk/ I miss the way that you smile/ I haven't seen it for a while.' It was so terrible and cheesy. I was so young, and it was probably the first song I wrote.

I even sold a few for chump change that were used in low-budget movies. They weren't always my greatest work, that's for sure. But those early songs helped me hone my songwriting chops and prepared me for professional-calibre songwriting once I'd got a major-label deal. That doesn't mean songwriting comes easily to me. If you ask my co-writers, they'll tell you I can make it a long, arduous process because I agonize over every note and every word. I compose the melodies, and other songwriters help me write the lyrics and different chord parts. Most of my songs have been written with David's daughter Amy Foster, who, as I've said, helped me write the lyrics for 'Home', but also for 'Everything' and, from my fourth album, 'Hold On' and 'Haven't Met You Yet'. They've all been hits.

My musical director and piano player, Alan Chang, is my other constant co-writing buddy. Alan supplies the chords and likes to tell me that my writing is too simple, that I should write something like Johnny Mandel's 'The Shadow Of Your Smile'. I love that song and its complexity, both lyrically and melodically, but it's just not in my DNA to write one like it.

I believe there's a simple thing we all hunger for, and I have no problem delivering that. We expect a certain note to follow, so I say give the listener that note. I'm a child of the Beatles and three-chord songs. They move me. There are songs like 'You And I' by Stevie Wonder, which I covered on my second record. The first time I heard it, I thought it was okay. But after five listens, it became beautiful to me. I could hear the nuances in it. As much as I appreciate that quality, it's not my songwriting approach. I want a pop song that hits you over the head, that doesn't sink in slowly. I need you to hear it three times and, next thing you know, you're in the shower and humming it.

That's where I'm at right now, anyway. Maybe one day I'll be more introspective and want to write more complicated, less accessible songs.

I've known Amy and Alan since the early days, so we have a super-comfortable rapport. Amy is especially comfortable arguing with me because we've been writing songs together since I was hanging out in LA, broke and begging for work. I'd go over to the house she shared with her husband and stay for dinner, chat for hours and, ultimately, we'd write rough versions of songs. We started to compose what became 'Everything' that way, although we recorded it many years later.

Amy has become like a sister to me, which means that no matter how heated our arguments get, there are never any hard feelings. A big joke between us is that we don't agree on words that are supposed to rhyme. What Amy calls a rhyme is not what I'd call a rhyme. She also pushes me to be honest in my lyrics, to take them to a personal place. As I've said, when I was writing 'Home' on the second album, I called her up and said I was having trouble getting the words right. Amy said I should touch on the pain of being away from Debbie, my girlfriend at the time. I was reluctant because I thought it would be too cheesy, but she argued that people would relate to a song that came straight from the heart. And she was right.

When we wrote 'Everything', the hit song from the third album, I'd originally penned a few lyrics about 'when I dream' or something like that. I just made up some words so that I could sing the melody – create what we call the 'la-la tape', usually with Alan playing piano. I give it to Amy so she can help me come up with some words. Then we go back and forth several times and I make lots of changes until we hammer the song into shape. Amy also writes novels, and she's a great writer, but I need to contribute to the lyrics because I'm the one who might be singing them for two hundred shows a year, year after year. If I don't believe in what I'm singing, it's just not going to work.

Another song on the third album, a ballad called 'Lost', I wrote with the great Canadian pop singer Jann Arden. Jann is a good friend of mine, and she's also managed by Bruce. I relate to her because we're both comedians who like to sing really sad ballads, which would seem like a contradiction. I think 'Lost' is one of my best songs, but judging from the numbers, the fans seem to like 'Hold On' better.

By now, in 2007, I had been a major-label artist for four years. When you sign to a major label, the world thinks your career doesn't start until the moment you put your pen to the record contract. So, in interviews, everybody would talk to me like I was some kind of newcomer who'd only been going four years – but I'd already been working for more than a decade and I felt like an old pro. That was why I took control of the third release. I did it in the nicest possible way, even though I wasn't always that nice about it.

making it big

By the time it came out, I was both excited and terrified because I truly thought I'd made the best record of my career, and I wondered if I could do any better. Even before it was released in May 2007, I knew that I was sitting on two more hit songs.

One day, Bruce informed me that I had sold around thirteen million records, including the DVDs and my Christmas EP. Only four years in, and thirteen million in sales made me proud. It validated me as an artist, giving me the confidence to believe more in my opinions and instincts. David Foster said I had interfered just enough. I'd brought the songs and, conceptually, I made it clear that each one was a story. To me, each song was like a movie. For example, if singer Donny Hathaway had ever sung 'That's Life' it would have been very soulful. Hathaway influences me stylistically, so when I covered the song, I wanted to make it an inspirational gospel tune rather than the famously guy's-guy version that Sinatra did. I also wanted to do Eric Clapton's 'Wonderful Tonight' as a bossa nova with Brazilian jazz genius Ivan Lins, in the spirit of the Frank Sinatra and Antonio Carlos Jobim duets.

I wanted to bring in Boyz II Men for the steamy 'Comin' Home Baby', even though other people wanted Destiny's Child for the song. They said, 'Destiny's Child has heat,' and reminded me that they'd had a string of hits. I responded that I didn't need someone else's heat, I just needed to make great songs. There has to be the right mix of people. Back on my second album, someone had suggested I use the then fifteen-year-old singer Renee Olstead for the duet 'Quando Quando Quando'. I said there was no way that a thirty-year-old man should be singing a love duet with a fifteen-year-old girl. I wanted Nelly Furtado, and if I didn't get Nelly, I wouldn't do the song. It was the same with Boyz II Men. If I didn't get those guys for the song, I would have nixed it entirely. Once I get an idea in my head, it's stuck there. You don't want to argue with me. I'll only get on your nerves. I love all the people who work with me, but I've got to do what I've got to do. My friends will tell you I can be really stubborn.

I'm stubborn because I believe I have a gut instinct for an appealing chord or lyric. If you play me a chord on the piano, I'll tell you if it conveys happiness, sadness, melancholy, hope, remorse, whatever. Many times I hear a song and think that its beautiful melody doesn't match the lyrics.

I've always loved to write songs, but I've never put pressure on myself to do so. Great singers such as Elvis Presley, Ella Fitzgerald, Bobby Darin and Frank Sinatra never wrote their own songs. They were brilliant interpreters. If you can tell a great story with your voice, your style, your phrasing, then you can do this for ever. Look at Tony Bennett. He's still going strong.

I have arguments with my co-writers because I'm not always good at working with people. I prefer to write the song on my own and bring in the co-writers later. I produce the melody, at least one good hook and maybe the first verse. I'm really lucky because I get to write a pop song for the radio and I also interpret these great American pop standards to make them my own. I can't think of any other artist out there who gets away with mixing the genres the way I've been allowed to.

Since I began my career, some well-intentioned people have advised me to stick to contemporary pop and forget the old stuff. Some have even tried to turn me into a singer who looks like he just walked out of the Backstreet Boys. I said a flat-out 'No' to all of them from the get-go. That's not who I am. Also, if I had started off as a contemporary pop singer, people would have called me a fraud if I'd then switched to the classics. My credibility as a singer of standards would be drawn into question. Even now, as much as I enjoy straddling both the new and the old, why would I do a complete 180-degree turn and become something I'm not?

Looking back at the release of that album in 2007, I remember I was still adjusting to the idea of relentless touring. As much as I love live performance, the grind did not come naturally to me. Back in those early days, I didn't have the luxury of giving myself a day off if I needed it. I had to go where the work was. I've learned several coping strategies since then, such as making sure I'm always in touch with my loved ones and taking regular breaks. In the early days, there were times I'd go home after being away for months and feel so detached, exhausted and self-centred that I just wanted to avoid everyone. I wasn't always nice to my family, even when my mom wanted me to come over for dinner. I was so tired I just wanted to be free of appointments and responsibilities, even family ones.

Bruce is a great manager, because he has foresight and he knows the business so well. He knew that I'd need to focus my energy on live performance if I wanted to be successful. He pushed me to tour and make television appearances even when I was so exhausted I got angry with him. When I was tired, he'd say, 'I know you're tired. But you've got to go to South Africa or Australia, kid. Don't stop now. Get to these markets. They'll be loyal, and when you're an old man, you can go back and sing there again.' Now that I see how the business has gone, I appreciate his foresight. Believe me, I wasn't so grateful back then. Bruce took the brunt of my frustration, my loneliness and my anger. If I argued too much, he'd bark, 'Don't be a wimp. Go out there and do it.'

I remember a particularly low point. I had just flown a twelve-hour red-eye from London to Vancouver. I'd gone to London to do a TV appearance, and I was happy to be home, because I only had a short break before I had to fly off to the US for some shows. The plane had just touched down when I got a call from Bruce. He said, 'Kid, we have a big show in the United Kingdom lined up. Do you want to do it?' I said of course I did. He said, 'That's great, because you have to get on another plane and fly back to London.' I didn't even have time to leave the airport. I was so tired and devastated I actually cried.

Another time, I was in Paris touring for my second album. Debbie and I had broken up and I wasn't sleeping. I wasn't feeling mentally strong at all. I was sitting in my hotel room feeling so run-down and depressed that I pulled out my laptop and started making plans for a trip to the Bahamas or some place where nobody could find me. I'd just disappear and no one would know. I'd be gone for two months. I didn't do it. But I was at breaking point. I hadn't seen my grandpa in months. I was missing out on seeing my nieces and nephews growing up. I thought, I don't need to do this any more. I've made a couple of million dollars. Enough is enough. Of course, no matter how bad it ever got, I've never bailed on anyone, because my need to please everyone is fortunately bigger than any moment of despair.

That brings me back to the attention I was receiving as a celebrity around this time. It was all so new to me and, like I said before, it was a major adjustment on top of everything else. Life was exciting. I remember sitting at the Academy Awards in Los Angeles: I was next to Anne Hathaway and behind Queen Latifah. I'd recently done a compilation of Ella Fitzgerald songs with Queen Latifah, Diana Krall, Natalie Cole and others. I didn't feel like one of them, exactly, but I was starting to relate to them as people. I remember meeting Tom Cruise at a party and thinking he was one of the nicest people I'd ever met. I entirely forgot he was a celebrity. My world was becoming surreal.

On the flipside, I'd done some interviews that had got me into hot water because I was too sarcastic, too jokey, or simply too bloody clever for my own good. I was getting a reputation as a bit of a party boy or ladies' man. The reality is never as exciting as the sensational tabloid stories. Honestly, I've always been a homebody. I find going to awards shows or walking red carpets to be so much anxiety it's not that much fun. My favourite thing is to watch hockey with my family, talk hockey with my grandpa, or cook with my sisters and their families. I'd rather be playing ping-pong than on a red carpet. My wife, Luisana Lopilato, who is a star in her native Argentina, values time spent with family as much as I do. I am not blown away by celebrity trappings, like being behind the red velvet rope at lavish parties and getting the best tables at restaurants.

David advised me early on not to talk to my friends about my new life. He said that, no matter what I say, it's going to come off like I'm bragging. But I have the same friends I had when I was a kid, and those guys won't allow me to get a big head. They're the first to tell me that they read a magazine interview I did and I sounded like a goof. They keep me in line.

One ongoing problem is that I'm unable to censor myself in interviews — maybe it's because I don't realize that not all reporters are my friends and that they're more interested in a good soundbite than what I really mean. I can say stupid things, but please don't hold me to it: I'm only human. And I'd rather be entertaining and silly than a boring stuffed shirt. But as a result of several interviews that have come back to haunt me, I no longer read anything that's written about me. I just don't have the stomach for it.

It seems that everybody wants to be famous, but when you make it happen, you may discover there's more bad to it than good. Around the time of that third album, I was feeling that the bad far outweighed the good. One thing I do like about being famous is that when I go to a party I'm no longer standing there like a lemon, making ridiculously nervous small-talk. Now we can skip all that. There's always a conversation starter.

don't
take
away
their
dignity

Some time after I'd made my second album, I was on a flight with my tour manager, Chris Chappel. We were seated in first class, and I had expensive Hugo Boss suits in a bag that I wanted to hang up. I handed them to the flight attendant in a way that sounded too much like a demand. They were worth something like ten thousand US dollars. I said, 'Could you hang these suits?' because they were going to get creased. Chris felt I was being rude. I always say that if I was twenty-one when success had happened, I would have been a nightmare. Looking back, an episode like that makes me cringe. Chris told me I'd acted like a diva. I'd embarrassed him. And he was absolutely right: I had behaved like a jerk. I spent the rest of the flight humiliated, feeling like the kind of person my parents had taught me not to be.

You get self-absorbed out of necessity, trying to survive this life. And when you come home, it's hard to sit down with everyone else, because you're used to doing what you want to do when you want to do it. There've been times when I've looked in the mirror and said, 'Get over yourself.' I have to remind myself to stay true to my roots, not to let my temper or my ego get the better of me. In 2007, I had released my third album, *Call Me Irresponsible*, and I was sitting with record sales of thirteen million. I was feeling cocky, and about to start promoting my world tour with appearances on big American daytime shows, like *Live With Regis & Kelly* and *Rachael Ray*. I had a big world tour coming up, with shows booked in arenas for the first time in my career. I was getting major radio play. I was riding high.

CBS Sunday Morning wanted to capture me shopping in my hometown, so I took them to a popular public market. I wanted to show them a soup place

don't take away their dignity

I love. I was bragging about it. So, we went up to the counter and I was about to order soup for the cameras, and the girl serving me said, 'Turn off your cameras, please. We don't allow cameras here.'

And I said, 'Listen, this is CBS, and I'm Michael Bublé, and all I'm doing is telling them that you're great. So don't trip about it. It's okay. It's the greatest soup. It's a huge amount of press, it's a huge TV show.'

And she said, 'I said, turn off the cameras.'

Oh, my God, I was angry. Me being me, instead of being the reasonable person and saying to the TV guy, 'Okay. Turn the camera off,' I said to the girl, 'What the hell? You guys are getting so much goddamn business that you don't need this gigantic TV show to come and have me testify to how great your soup is? I'm sorry, big shots, sorry you're doing so well.'

She said, basically, 'My boss doesn't want your TV exposure, so go away.'

I said, 'Tell your boss he's a f****** idiot.' Yep. That was me. Such a brilliant guy. And they kicked us out of the market. That's right. They kicked us out. They called security. And I hated myself for two days after that. Couldn't I just have said, 'Shut off the camera,' and walked away? I can't think how many times I've said to myself, 'Ah, man, I'm a jerk.' I've had such anxiety because I've been rude. It bothers me for days. I think that talking about it to people, even reporters, somehow makes me feel better – like, if I admit it out loud I'm learning to be a better man.

The Internet and cell-phone technology have really made it difficult for people who've achieved a bit of fame. Everybody can know what you're doing within nanoseconds of you doing it. One time, when I was home in Vancouver with Luisana, we were out shopping and dropped into a lingerie store. We noticed some people watching us, and we smiled and kept walking. We ended up at a Starbucks coffee shop and within minutes people were surrounding us, literally lined up for autographs. I got a phone call from my mother and she said, 'I hear you were shopping for lingerie.'

I asked her, 'How do you know that? Are you in the mall somewhere?' and I started to look around.

She said, 'No, I heard it on the radio.'

I couldn't believe it. When I told Lu, she said, *'Amore*, look outside the window.' And I looked up, and there were paparazzi taking pictures of us. Stuff like that just freaks me out.

Another time, while I was on tour, I was walking through a shopping mall with friends and we stopped to watch a girls' choir that was singing. Suddenly one of them spotted me, screamed my name, and the entire choir rushed towards me and smothered me. I was almost buried under a pile of girls. My assistant and my friend from the record label were doing their best to help me get out from under them, which, you can imagine, wasn't easy. They were screaming, 'Let him breathe, let him breathe!' I think they were actually worried I might suffocate to death.

Of course, the fans meant well. They were just excited girls. I've felt the way they did then towards an artist I admire, although I never trampled anyone. It was tremendously flattering.

A more sinister episode happened early on, when I was playing to about ten thousand people in the state of Virginia. I was at a place called the Wolf Trap and I was in the crowd and I heard this screaming. I turned around and the first thing I saw was a fist swinging towards me. I ducked and had enough time to put my hand on the guy's chin and just push him away from me. I didn't have security at the time, and it's because of guys like him that I have a bodyguard in the crowds with me today.

I didn't think much more about it, and I got back on to the stage, but the guy came running at me, this time with wire wrapped around his hands, like he was going to strangle me. A bunch of people pulled him away and he was arrested by the FBI. I heard later that he was so irate he tried to kick out the rear window inside the car. It turned out he believed that I had stolen music from black people and I deserved to die. I didn't press charges because I didn't want any more to do with him.

Another time, I was walking along a downtown street in Vancouver, just doing some shopping. I was standing at a street corner when a guy came up to me and said, 'You're Michael Bublé? You deserve an upper cut, you f****** jerk. You stole my song "Home". I wrote that song with my buddy.' The guy had a liquor-store bag and looked like he was going to clock me with an unopened bottle. He made a jerking motion towards me with it, and I instinctively punched him in the nose. He ran into a nearby bookstore and I pursued him. I was really angry that he could threaten me like that. He ran up the escalator inside the store and screamed, 'Hey, everybody, Canada's favourite crooner is trying to kill me!' I yelled at him to be a man, that he couldn't just threaten someone and run off, but I could see it was a lost battle. I walked home shaking, I was so upset. I felt really bad that I'd lost my temper and caused a scene. I guess you can take the boy out of Burnaby but you can't take Burnaby out of the boy.

By the way, those episodes are the exceptions. Almost everybody is really nice to me when I meet them. They are so laid-back and sweet. But because of those weird situations, I can get a little gun-shy, too, when people walk up to me on the street. I don't know what to expect. But I don't want a wall between me and my audience. I want to be able to interact and meet my fans. It's one of the best things about this job.

don't take away their dignity

One thing I can't stand is when a security person, or anyone else, thinks they're doing me a favour by being rude to a fan. They'll ask, 'Are you all right with this person?' right in front of them, and I'll say, 'Of course. It's fine.' I'm extremely embarrassed by this type of élitist treatment. I feel badly because people should always remember not to take away someone's dignity. You can crush someone really easily, and it might seem like a mere moment to you, but to them it will stick for a lifetime, the pain, the embarrassment. We should all be sensitive to our potential to hurt someone. And, really, so what if I have to put up with a drunk person blabbing away to me about what my music means to them, and how their little sister likes to dance to 'Quando Quando Quando'? It's a small price to pay for having fans who are willing to spend their money on my records. I'm not being a martyr, I'm just being fair.

It reminds me of all the times when I was young and I'd get dressed up nicely and go downtown to this nightclub where lots of hot girls would hang out. This was way before I'd had a taste of fame. I'd be waiting in line, and it could be totally dead, and the bouncer would say, 'No. You can't go in.'

I'd say, 'Screw you. Who do you think you are? You think I need to come to your shit club so bad?'

That kind of thing would really get my back up. I still have those moments, too, even now that I have money – although today I'm more likely to get access. There was a time in London, when I was staying in the upscale Trafalgar Hotel, and I wanted to go to the bar, called the Rockwell. I'd left my hotel key with the valet, and the Rockwell bouncer said I couldn't get in without it. I was livid. He wouldn't let me in, probably because I look young. I said, 'I'm staying at this hotel. You have got to let me in,' and took a step towards the entrance. He stepped in front of me. I said, 'Fifty-four people are staying at this hotel and I'm paying for those fifty-four people. Now, you let me in and get your hands off me.' I just couldn't take it.

I'm not the sort of guy who demands champagne to be waiting for him on his arrival, but I can't stand to be confronted by prejudice. Look at where I come from. We're not trailer trash, but at one point I didn't know which fork to use, and it made me a bit insecure. If I'm paying for a hotel, if I'm paying good money, don't make me feel like I'm something stuck to the bottom of your shoe.

I've also been protective of my girlfriends over the years and, of course, of my wife, Luisana. I won't let anybody treat my girl like a second-class citizen. I remember I was dating someone who was snubbed while she was trying to buy a piece of jewellery at an expensive store in Los Angeles. She asked how much it cost, and the assistant responded, 'If you have to ask, I guess it's too much.'

My girlfriend said, 'All right,' and walked out.

Well, I was furious when I heard what had happened. Of course, I went right back into that store and I said to the clerk, 'What is wrong with you? My girlfriend came in here. I have enough money. But because you were a rude, pompous jerk, you lost the sale. Think about it the next time, and don't judge us because we come in wearing jeans and we're young.'

She said, 'Sorry, sir.'

I said, 'I'm sorry for you, because I can't imagine how many times a day you do it and you don't even know you're doing it.'

As I've said, I'm a guy with a temper. It's nothing like when I was a kid. It's just one of those things about me. It takes a lot to get me angry, but when I do, I can blow. The CBS journalist who was doing that piece in the public market took me aside and said, 'I like you a lot, but what are you doing? You can't do that, Michael. The ten things you've done that are great are erased in one moment because those two people who saw you are going to tell fifty people what a dick you are.' There are days when I wish I could be more like my dad. That low-key guy, so patient, no temper . . . I'm way more like my mom. I'm fiery. We're Italian.

I was never a great student, and I never felt like a genius. But I am learning that you don't have to be smart at math to be good in business. If you know what you want and can talk to people, you can achieve things in life. Sometimes I worry that I'm coming over as opportunistic or manipulative. But, on the other hand, I may simply be seen as diplomatic.

My father, for example, has a brilliantly diplomatic way: he knows how to make everyone around him happy. He's a great boss and leader type of guy, and my role model. When I was around nine or ten years old, my father wanted to throw out our hot-water tank because it was old. There must have been some city scheme to get rid of old hot-water tanks because a lot of people in the neighbourhood were throwing them out. My father took me up to the beer and wine store, and bought a case of beer. On garbage pick-up day, he put the hot-water tank out on the street with the beer and a note that said, 'If you can take it, thanks, boys. If not, enjoy the brew.' He knew the garbage guys. And our hot-water tank was the only one that got picked up that morning. Everybody else had to take theirs to the dump and pay way more than a case of beer cost.

I know my dad and he wouldn't have been disappointed if they'd said they couldn't take it. His whole lesson to me was that it takes nothing to be thoughtful towards other people.

You don't rob people of their dignity. For example, I don't like posing for photos at the best of times, even when it's a professional photographer who's taking the pictures. If someone on the street asks me to pose, I'll say no. Then, unfortunately, they feel really stupid and embarrassed for asking. So, I'll immediately follow with, 'Please don't take it personally. It's just that if I pose for photos then inevitably they end up on the Internet, and I look stupid or ugly. How about I call your sister and say hello? I could sign your shopping bag. Whatever you want.'

When you get a little famous, you have to be very sensitive to other people, because you can easily forget. Paul Anka is really good at interacting with his fans. We'll be out for dinner and a fan will come up to the table and say hello, and he'll say warmly, 'Thank you so much. It's great to meet you. Enjoy your night.' The conversation is over. The fan who came up to say hello walks away feeling good, and Paul gets to enjoy his dinner and his privacy without feeling like a jerk. It's a fine balance, and he's mastered it.

By the way, as an aside, I do a terrific Paul Anka impersonation. I could probably have been an impersonator in another life.

There are other celebrities, however, who don't have the same deft touch that Paul has. I don't want to mention any names, but there was this big actor at the Grammys, and I saw a kid come up to him and ask for a picture. The actor shut the kid down like he was dropping a brick on his head. He said very coldly, 'I don't feel like it right now.' I watched that kid walk away and my heart sank for him. I didn't understand how anyone could be so mean to another person. That kid must have had his perception of the actor completely shattered by that one embarrassing episode. All the actor had to do was put his hand on the kid's shoulder and say, 'You know what, kiddo? It's really nice to meet you, but I don't pose for pictures. I'm sorry.'

It would have cost him nothing.

And it's that easy – it all comes back to the fact that it's easy to be kind and respectful to others. It's not rocket science, and there's no excuse for being rude. I have extended this mindset to members of my staff, including my manager, who has a different approach. Bruce is notoriously blunt with people, mostly because he doesn't have time to waste dancing around the task at hand. Also, he likes to share his opinions on local politics and current events on a popular radio show he does in Vancouver. In Vancouver, Bruce is as much a celebrity as I am. I know that his tough exterior is a bit of shtick and the man has a soft side, but the rest of the world isn't aware of that. I've had conversations with Bruce, David and other members of my team and told them that yelling at people and being rude is not part of the game plan. Not as long as I'm paying the bills.

It's a conundrum, the fame thing. You can be hungry for it – and, let's face it, it's imperative that you're hungry for it if you're ever going to get it – and then, once you have it, it can weigh on you heavily. I'll never forget the people who were there for me. It's not just about protecting the feelings of strangers, but family and friends, too.

I feel guilty that I can't spend more time and energy on the people who cared for me on my way up, people like my first manager, Bev. I seldom see her now simply because of my relentless tour schedule. I'll phone and text my old friends when I can, such as on Christmas Day, but every spare hour I have when I'm not working is so precious that I can't properly catch up with most of the old gang any more. That's a major downside to success.

There's also the fact that paparazzi follow you everywhere, looking for that one super-embarrassing shot that will snare them a pay cheque. As I said earlier, the misinformation spread around the Internet scares me. I think of it as a minefield that I have to navigate on a daily basis. I'll do an interview with a newspaper reporter and make some off-the-cuff remark, and the next morning I'll see it spread around the Internet but twisted into something controversial. I know that controversy makes for good headlines, but it can feel like such a betrayal to be used in that way.

I was misquoted after I announced to Kathie Lee Gifford and Hoda Kotb on NBC's *Today* show that Luisana and I were to be married on 6 April 2011. I jokingly made reference to the wedding of Prince William and Kate Middleton. I said, 'I was going to do it on the twenty-ninth but I figured they wouldn't get any press.' And if the media had quoted me the exact way I'd said it, the joke would have been clear to everyone. Instead I was quoted with one word changed that drastically altered my meaning. The quote that ran was: 'I was going to do it on the twenty-ninth, but I figured I wouldn't get any press,' which made it look like I'm such an egomaniac that I'd actually be worried about being overshadowed by the royal wedding. This was the perfect example of how one word change can completely misconstrue a quote and make me look like a jerk. It drives me nuts, and it happens more often than you'd think. That attempt to generate negative publicity where there was none really made me think that, when it came to the press, there was no winning.

On the upside, the fans who know my work seem to be unfazed by the tabloid silliness, so I'm thankful for that. It has made me more cautious, though. I'm less inclined to be so frank with the media these days. I'm particularly careful with comments about my family and people close to me. I don't want them to get hurt in this crazy game of celebrity. Luisana and I have made it a policy not to discuss our relationship in public: sharing such personal details with the world would be the quickest way to destroy it.

crazy
in
love

The making of my fourth album, *Crazy Love*, was meaningful for a couple of reasons. I pushed to make a record that was more authentic-sounding than my previous recordings, and I had fallen in love with Luisana Lopilato.

I first laid eyes on her backstage after a show in Buenos Aires, where I'd played at the famous Gran Rex Theatre. I was walking with my grandpa and a security guard to a waiting van when I saw Lu standing about forty feet away. I was feeling very down, very lonely, and I said to my grandpa, 'That is the most beautiful woman I've ever seen in my life.' As we drove off, I added, 'And I will never see her again.'

Later, as Fate would have it, I met Lu again while I was sitting with my grandpa and my uncle Butch at a bar. The show's promoter came over and asked if I'd like to meet two of Argentina's biggest actors. I'd had a few drinks and said, 'Sure, whatever.' In walked Lu with this incredibly handsome actor named Rodrigo. He could speak English, and Lu couldn't, so I ended up talking to him for most of the night. I assumed they were a couple and, of course, I didn't want to hit on his girlfriend. Little did I know that Lu was texting her mother a message that said, 'I think Michael Bublé must be gay.' Later, once we were engaged, I would tell that story at my shows.

I finally asked Rodrigo if they were together, and when he said, 'No', I thought, Oh, my God. This is incredible. I invited them out and Lu's sister came along, and she knew a little English, which helped us communicate. Susan Leon, my good friend from Warner Bros Records, was also with us. I said to her, 'If this girl falls in love with me, I'm going to marry her.'

She said, 'I know. This is it, isn't it, Michael?'

Seven months later, in August 2009, I had finished *Crazy Love* and was doing promotional interviews. I remember telling a reporter friend in Vancouver that I had met the girl I planned on marrying. I was that sure.

On 9 October, a couple of months later, Oprah Winfrey launched my record by inviting me to appear on her show to sing my third number-one hit, 'Haven't Met You Yet'. My other two number ones were 'Home' and 'Everything'. It was a great time in my life, and I finally felt truly fulfilled and happy.

Crazy Love may be my most autobiographical album yet, not because the songs are directly about my life but because they spoke to me on a personal level. The only song from the album that didn't fit this theme, 'Georgia On My Mind', was intended as a tribute to Ray Charles, who will for ever own it. I included it on the album to keep the song alive for Ray, for the fans.

A lot of songs these days are recorded to perfection. Thanks to technology, songs can come out sounding glistening and shiny, as if they were manufactured by machines instead of people. It has an odd effect on the ear. We feel instinctively that something is not quite right, although we may not realize why. When I made the record, I decided I wanted to go back in time and record the songs live, with the backing singers and musicians in the room with me so that the vocals would bleed into the strings and the strings would bleed into the trumpet, and there would be all sorts of little flaws that are natural to old-time recordings. It's closer to the sound you'd hear when seeing a band live: all of those imperfections infuse it with depth and complexity. That depth gives a recording warmth, because it's man-made, not manufactured.

When I finished the album, I remember listening to it and saying to Dion Singer, from Warner Bros Records, that it felt entirely different from my previous recordings. I couldn't express to him what that difference was, but he knew instantly. Dion has been a major ally and adviser throughout every album I've made. I value and respect his opinions. He said to me, 'Music is not notes. Those are just noise. It's the space between the notes, it's the air in between, that makes it music.' That was a little epiphany for me because someone had finally articulated what I already understood at an instinctive level. The problem with modern technology is that it sucks the life out of music. A recording is put on an MP3 file and it's compressed till it's flat and lifeless, all the air has been sucked out. To the human ear, it just sounds wrong.

I was on a mission with *Crazy Love* to recapture that warm old sound, to set up microphones in the studio, to open the doors and let the sounds meld together, to have an edge and the vibe that I need to listen to those records.

Before we started recording, I conveyed this mission to David, sitting in a fancy steak restaurant in Vancouver. He was opposed to the idea. It wasn't his style. He preferred polished productions, nothing raw or organic. I said, 'Bullshit. You're the most brilliant music person I've met in my life. You can leave your comfort zone.' I convinced him and he came around.

I am surrounded by incredibly opinionated people who will argue with me, no matter how successful I become, and that's exactly how I want it. I will hear them out but, ultimately, if I have my mind set on something, we'll do it my way. Randy Berswick, who's part of my management team and oversees my tour production, admires my courage in covering iconic songs by Van Morrison, the Beatles and Ray Charles. He and Bruce think I'm crazy going there, but they can't help admiring it. I consider myself an interpreter, and there will never be only one interpretation of a song, no matter how great it is. My audience loves hearing those songs, too.

So, for *Crazy Love*, I brought Humberto in to mike everything differently from our previous albums. We worked on one of my favourite songs, 'Stardust', at Bryan Adams's Warehouse Studio in downtown Vancouver. My grandfather, who loved that song, had recorded it for me on my tape recorder and, as a boy, I'd play it over and over while I went to sleep. At the Warehouse, the a cappella group Naturally 7, from Atlanta, Georgia, and I sang with the rhythm section in the same room. We sang take after take and, like I said before, my family spent a whole day hanging out and listening to us, with my grandfather moved to tears at me singing his favourite song. I had a blast singing with the Naturally 7 guys, precisely because we were together in the same room, singing harmony like they would have back in the old days.

When I began doing press for the album, it struck me how the female reporters were divided from the male reporters as to which songs they liked best. The women almost always preferred Billy Vera's 'At This Moment', a heartrending ballad about a guy who's lost his woman's love. And they also liked the duet I did with Canadian songwriter Ron Sexsmith, 'Whatever It Takes'. We set his pop song to a bossa nova rhythm, and turned it into the hidden track. The guys, on the other hand, really connected with the sad ballad 'End Of May', which was a very difficult song for me to record. I had to stop several times because it had such personal meaning for me. It's a song about a romance that has ended, and it's poignant because it's filled with detailed imagery that captures the day-to-day experience of love, as well as the loss of it.

I may seem like a goofball jokester and guy's guy, but I can be really sensitive and sentimental, too. Lu is the stronger one in our relationship, seriously. I'm like the girl – I can be in tears at little things she does. When I try to convey my love to her, she'll look at me blankly and respond, 'Hey, I have a sore foot.' She makes me laugh. She has no patience with sentimentality, and likes to make fun of my mushy side.

crazy in love

My team did not immediately embrace the Sexsmith tune. They didn't get it. I also had to fight for 'At This Moment', which is now a big hit with my live audiences. David produced half the record in Los Angeles, including the heavily orchestrated 'Cry Me A River', 'All Of Me', 'Georgia On My Mind', 'All I Do Is Dream Of You', the Eagles' 'Heartache Tonight' and the Sexsmith tune. Humberto produced the classics 'Stardust' and 'You're Nobody Till Somebody Loves You'. And Bob Rock, famous for producing Metallica and Bon Jovi, sat in the producer's chair for my cover of Van Morrison's 'Crazy Love', Brook Benton's tune 'Baby (You've Got What It Takes)', which we recorded in New York with Sharon Jones of the Dap Kings, as well as two of my own songs, 'Hold On' and 'Haven't Met You Yet'. Bob has worked on other records with me over the years, and we have a great connection, an easygoing rapport. My nickname for Bob is 'the Dude' because he's more like a close buddy than a co-worker. He reminds me of Jeff Bridges' character in *The Big Lebowski*, minus the pot. We complement each other and he gets that authentic sound I'm always striving to make.

For 'Hold On', I wanted Bryan Adams to come in and supply his gravelly vocal for harmony. I thought it would be the perfect juxtaposition to my own voice. We went to a Canucks game and I asked him, 'Dude, would you do this for me?' And he said, sure. He's a cool, laid-back guy and we've become good friends. I wrote 'Hold On' on piano, which is a strange thing for me because I barely play. But I picked out the notes and came up with the melody.

Of course, 'Haven't Met You Yet' was a complete departure for me, because it veered off entirely from the swing jazz tunes I'd become famous for. But I've always had a penchant for writing pop songs, and I'm only now getting the chance to show that side of me. My co-writers will also tell you that I have a natural ability for writing country music, so I'll probably continue to diversify on future albums. It's not unusual for an artist to borrow from many styles. Anyone who knows Ray Charles's repertoire is aware that he straddled soul, gospel, country and pop.

Usually when I'm recording an album, I'll come up with nine or ten songs, then have to find a couple more to round out the record. However, with *Crazy Love*, I had so many songs I had to start cutting them, which was a painful process. David wanted to lose 'At This Moment' and 'Stardust' and make a shorter record, but I was determined to keep those songs.

I decided to omit 'End Of May', and I really came to regret it. But I knew I would find a place for the song somewhere, because I truly believe it's one of the finest recordings I've ever made. Someone suggested it could be a bonus track, but I thought it was too good for that. I wanted to save it for a soundtrack or my next record.

A Seattle singer-songwriter named Tim Seely composed the song and, incredibly, he was only nineteen when he wrote it. I found it through my musical director Alan Chang, who knew Tim. Tim had had a heart attack at the age of thirty-two, and he heard about our recording while he was in recovery. Like I said, the song was intensely personal for me, and emotionally, I found it hard to sing because it took me back to a tough time in my life. We kept the arrangement super-simple, just like Seely's original version, and released it separately on my *Hollywood the Deluxe* EP, along with another song that didn't make the record, which would become my fifth single, 'Hollywood'. 'Hollywood' is a catchy pop tune, but it didn't fit thematically with the rest of the album.

I co-wrote 'Hollywood' with the piano player I'd worked with in Toronto, when I'd played shows at a club there. His name is Robert Scott. It's a song about disillusionment with the celebrity culture we live in, and how sensational behaviour has replaced artistry – artists used to be singers, dancers, actors, comedians, choreographers, writers and directors. Sometimes, when I'm on a red carpet, I see people on that carpet with me who definitely did not get there because of any discernible talent. Rather, they are famous for being famous.

Crazy Love was not a cheap record to make. The symphony orchestra on 'Cry Me A River' alone cost $100,000. Also, because I wanted that old-school sound, it took a lot of time to make, and I worked with my producers for months on end. That album took longer to record than any other I'd made. I worked with David, for example, for three straight months. We recorded in the basement studio of the iconic Capitol Records building in Los Angeles – it looks like a stack of records. It is a fantastic place to work because the white walls are lined with photos of all the legends who've recorded there — Sinatra, Dean Martin, Judy Garland, Nat King Cole. I worked ten-hour days in the same labyrinth of studio rooms where Sinatra hung out. I recorded in Studio B, next door to Studio A, where Sinatra recorded in 1956. Throughout these sessions, David and I would jokingly call each other vulgar names, as we often do, much to the confusion and amusement of everybody around us.

When it was my turn to sing, I'd take a breath on my inhaler because I have slight asthma, pop a lozenge into my mouth and head into the booth. David would say something to the piano player such as, 'Do it like Vince Guaraldi', the jazz pianist best known for his work in composing pieces for the *Peanuts* comic strip. David would lean back in his chair, wearing his trademark Converse running shoes, feet up on the console, eyes closed, grooving to the music. After I'd nailed 'Pennies From Heaven', which we had briefly considered including, he said, 'It's far from bad. You swing harder than anybody I've met.' We'd end each day by going out for dinner and sitting around, reviewing our progress. I'd then drive to my rented Hollywood Hills house and put my feet up by the pool, listening to songs I had written on my laptop. I'm always working on some song on my laptop.

My surroundings were hilariously L.A. The house looked like the set for a porn video, with a sunken circular living room, palm tree in the middle, and black granite everywhere. The bathroom walls were covered from floor to ceiling with mirrors. The house wasn't exactly inspirational for creativity.

David has a big white-walled apartment in Malibu, where we also recorded part of the album. I love working there because it's so comfortable. Whitney Houston had been working there with David just before me, on her 2009 album, *I Look To You*, which was her first to go to number one since *The Bodyguard*.

When I'd finished the record, I truly believed it was the best I'd ever made. I know that's a cliché thing to say, that your most recent record is your best, but I believed it to the extent that I considered not doing interviews because I didn't think it needed promotion. Of course, the world doesn't work that way. Everything needs promotion.

I started doing press in the late summer of 2009, and by now I'd learned to be more careful with what I said to reporters. My relationship with Lu was in full swing, but I didn't talk about it the way I had with previous relationships. Because Lu is a star in Argentina, though, I did get bombarded with questions from pushy reporters who wanted a quote or a photo of me with her. I learned to shut them down. Lu is used to media attention. The paparazzi hound her in Argentina. When we were dating, she'd just released a hit Spanish-language film called *Dad for a Day*, which was bigger there than *Harry Potter and the Half-Blood Prince*.

We both know that if you start sharing personal information with the public and giving it away, it's not yours any more. Your relationship becomes tabloid fodder. Also, the more you speak about your private life, the more people expect you to speak about it. So, for the first time in my life when I was doing interviews, I would say, 'You know what? Ask me about anything else, but I want to keep that part of my life private.'

I'd been through a lot of heartache and seriously dark periods in my life, which had served me well on that album. I'd been forced to face my insecurities and weaknesses, to become a better man. I had more focus. I was living in the present. I was mentally and physically stronger. On previous records, I'd been reckless with my voice and my body, not taking care of myself, not working out. But I was in good shape while making *Crazy Love*. I felt good.

As a consequence, I had a lot of fun making the videos for the record. As in almost every other aspect of my career, I had taken more control of the video-making process too. For 'Haven't Met You Yet', I sent a treatment of the video idea I had to a high-profile director named Brett Ratner, whom I'd met at a dinner party. He absolutely loved the idea, a cross between an Offspring music video and a scene from the movie *Ferris Bueller's Day Off*, which has always struck a chord with me. I loved that movie as a kid, particularly the scene where Ferris is on a float in a massive parade, singing 'Twist and Shout'.

My launch point for the idea came from watching the Offspring video for 'Why Don't You Get a Job?'. In it, singer Dexter Holland walks through town with a marching band. Amy suggested I use a marching band in a supermarket. I thought that the store would come alive once a bachelor guy comes in to buy frozen pizza and other bachelor food and spots this amazing girl. The supermarket turns into an old-time musical, with the shop assistants and old people dancing, a marching band and the parking lot full of people dancing. Of course, at the end, it all turns out to be a big fantasy, and the girl of his dreams walks into the store and saunters right past the guy.

However, because of budget constraints and scheduling issues, Brett couldn't direct the video. I was getting pretty frustrated trying to find a director. I remember I was at a photo shoot for the *Crazy Love* album cover, and I was sitting on a patio on a conference call with my management team. They put this guy, Rich Lee, on the phone. Rich had an impressive resumé. He had directed videos for Eminem, Lady Gaga and the Black Eyed Peas, but we'd never talked before. Bruce thought he might be the guy for the job. Rich said, 'Hey, man, I think we should do this and this and this.' He had all these ideas.

I was almost rude, to be honest. I said, 'No. With all due respect, this is not a collaboration, this is me telling you what I want. I'll explain from the start. The music starts up and I'm pushing a buggy with a shaky wheel. I want a camera underneath the buggy . . . ' and on I went. I already had every scene worked out in my head.

If you ask anybody who works with me, I'm quite confident in my ideas, and might even be a control freak.

Rich said he thought it was a cool idea and that I had a strong concept. He was surprised that I had the whole treatment already figured out so well. We began to work together, and I liked his ideas, such as having the fantasy girl and me on a bed rolling down the aisles, or the two of us in a spinning phone booth. He also had the idea that we should contact choreographer Kenny Ortega, who had done the dance sequence in *Ferris Bueller's Day Off*. He called him and said I loved that dance scene and would he mind if we used the choreography from it? He said to go for it. So, the choreography from that movie is the same choreography in my video.

I wanted the part of the fantasy girl to be played by Lu, but she was unavailable, filming a movie in Argentina. People started throwing the names of Hollywood actresses at me, but I felt insecure about working with someone

I didn't know. But then Lu's director gave her a day off and she managed to fly all the way from Argentina, arrive at five a.m., shoot in one day, and fly back to Argentina.

We shot the video over two days at a supermarket not far from where I grew up. Rich and I worked together really well. We trusted each other, and I loved the way it turned out, which isn't usually the case with my videos. My early videos were concepts supplied by other directors, and not all of them successful.

It was the wee hours of the morning, we were standing outside and it was still dark. All the lights were set up, there were about three hundred extras, and the confetti machines started to blow. I was watching money being spent in every direction. Bruce was with me, and I turned to him and said, 'We did it.' It was one of the proudest moments of my life because I knew that it would alter the course of my career and change my image. I had been stuck in a pigeonhole for so long, as the throwback singer with the older audience. This video, in which I wore casual clothes instead of a suit and sang a pop song, changed how people would see me. I went from wearing a suit to wearing a pair of jeans, from being the Sinatra guy to a young kid doing a pop song. The song went to number one. It all came together, pop song and video.

With the release of that video and the pop singles, my demographic has changed. About three years ago, I'd see a university-age girl in my audience and be surprised. Now my audiences are routinely one-third university age, both guys and girls, and the gay community comes out more too. As well, I'm seeing more husbands and boyfriends, and they're clearly not dragged to my shows, like they used to be. It gives me great material to work with. I always single out a hubby type in the front row and hit on him a bit for a laugh.

The 'Hollywood' video was a turning point for me where videos are concerned. It made me realize that I should never do anything that I don't feel strongly about. For example, I was told I needed to do a video for my second single, 'Hold On', which had become a hit. It was a big rush, and I came up with some ideas, but I was too busy to choose a treatment I really loved. I went with one that had me skating on an ice rink, which I didn't like so much, but I trusted the director. We spent around $200,000 on the video, but when I saw it I said I'd never release it. It was terrible. It was so cheesy it took me right back to the embarrassment I'd felt with my early videos, the ones that seem so middle-of-the-road now when I look at them. I learned a valuable lesson: that I should never settle for something that I don't believe in 100 per cent.

That's why, when it came time to do the video for 'Hollywood', I was involved in every creative decision. I called up Bruce and told him I had an idea – I wanted to play myself as narrator, but I also wanted to play myself as a bunch of different characters. A hair-metal rocker. A teenage idol. A Hollywood icon.

I even envisaged dressing up as Lady Gaga or a blonde starlet. But my record label was worried that it would taint my image. They thought it was too much like an Eminem video. Someone suggested I simply get a bunch of Hollywood celebrities to play themselves while I performed for them. Of course I thought that was a lame idea. I called Bruce again and insisted that I wanted to stick with my idea, and he said to go for it. I told him it would cost around $500,000 to make, and he checked with the label. They were already reluctant, and they balked at the price, offering to spend only $200,000. I believed so much in my idea that I paid the balance out of my own pocket.

I enlisted Rich Lee as my director and, once again, he completely understood my concept – which was a spoof on celebrity culture and my comment on how ridiculous it can be. I played a James Dean-type character and the aforementioned hair-metal rocker. I also impersonated fellow Canadian Justin Bieber, lounging in a talk-show chair, wearing a blue hoodie, with big bangs swept across my forehead. At one point, I considered Miley Cyrus, but decided to stick with an impersonation of the Bieb. I met Justin not long after releasing the video and he hadn't seen it. He just reached out and gave me a big hug, saying, 'We Canadians stick together.' Sweet kid.

As I've said, I've always loved doing impersonations. I impersonate practically everyone around me. I'd done a lot as a kid at acting school, and I find it pretty easy to inhabit a role quickly. Although music videos don't have speaking parts, I still consider it acting because you have to convey emotion. We shot the video in two intense seventeen-hour days in Los Angeles. For the very last shot, I brought in my best friend Carsten and my brothers-in-law to appear in a convertible car with me. I flew them down just for that shot, and they loved it.

I had a blast making those videos. I may not be quite where I want to be yet professionally, because there are so many things I want to do, but I'm realizing exactly what I want.

my
life
now

Career-wise, my life is now a lot about repetition. It goes like this. Record an album. Promote it. Tour for two years. Repeat. There is a rhythm to my life now, and it's been steadily gaining momentum. I have changed since those early years. I'm much more confident and comfortable with my job, which is hugely freeing, especially creatively. When you are intimidated by people or feeling like an imposter, it's a creative setback. At the same time, it's important that I never get too cocky for my own good, because that can be the kiss of death to an artist.

When I first started out, David made a video tape of me promising never to turn into an arrogant jerk, because he'd seen that happen too many times. That videotape is his way of holding me to my promise that I'll never become that guy. And I don't think I will ever turn into the jerk celebrity who thinks his life is the most interesting one in the room. For one thing, my family won't let me. For another, the fame-and-fortune thing is fun, but I don't define myself by it. I'm happy with my life because I've found my comfort zone. I have confidence. I've found my groove. I've read the allegorical novel *The Alchemist,* by Brazilian writer Paulo Coehlo; it examines how the universe conspires to make things happen when you know what you really want. I truly believe that's how life works.

When I record, I am intensely involved with my producers and my musicians. It is relaxed, easy, creative and satisfying, even though the days are long.

When I am promoting the album, I sit in hotel rooms to talk to press from all around the world, repeating answers to the same questions asked over and over. After a while, I get my stories down pat, fine-tuning my soundbites with precision efficiency. If I like a journalist, they get an honest and revealing interview. If I feel they haven't done their research or they're looking for dirt, they get the pat answers.

Television appearances are pretty easy. They don't require that much of you, except for a few upbeat comments and knowing when to let the host talk. I have even filled in for Paul O'Grady on his popular British talk-show and had a great time doing it.

Going on the road is the most gruelling part of the job, but I was born to do it. Friends who come with me for a few days wonder how I can handle not seeing daylight. There are days I spend entirely underground in the back of an arena before the show. Once the show is over, I go directly to a waiting tour bus and travel all night. I'll wake up in another underground loading bay in some other arena and start all over again. It's like living in a cocoon. There are days when I get tired or irritable, but if I start acting like a diva and complaining too much, the only one who hurts is me. Besides, for the most part, I do love it. Like I said, I was born for this job. Even the motion of the tour bus reminds me of sleeping on my father's fishing boat. I find it soothing.

Let me give you a glimpse of my day-to-day life now, when I'm on the road with my seventy-strong crew and the days blur together until I've lost all concept of time. The way I see it, we operate like a factory or a steel mill, ticking along until show time, when the factory closes down for a couple of hours, then wakes up again and ticks along to the next city.

I'm backstage in Grand Rapids, Michigan, where I've played several times before, although I've never gone far beyond the arena. I'm nervous about a big hockey game between the Vancouver Canucks and their arch rivals, the Chicago Blackhawks. It has special meaning also because I play Chicago the next night, so I'll be face to face with an audience full of Blackhawks fans. More importantly, however, the Blackhawks knocked the Canucks out of the play-offs the year before and won the Stanley Cup, which hurt. I'm worrying that I won't be able to see a lot of the game because I'm about to go on stage.

I'm seated in my dressing room a half-hour before show time. It's another blank bunker with grey walls and a nondescript couch. Nearby are the two stuffed toys I take with me everywhere, like good-luck tokens. My nephew O'Shae gave me Kermit the Frog and Lu gave me the stuffed pig because she thinks it has my eyes. She calls me 'cochinito', which means 'little pig'.

Holly is airbrushing my face with a light coat of stage makeup. On my dressing-table are the usual supplies, my inhaler, allergy medication, a bottle of Tam Dao cologne. My screensaver on my computer is a close-up of Lu's face when she was a kid. I watch the game on my laptop and reluctantly take my eyes away to get dressed for the show. My wardrobe containers are in another room, where other members of my crew steam out the creases in my clothes and keep them ready for stage and photo opportunities. Holly brings me my shirt, and I get into it as I keep one eye on the game. Only when my guitarist enters the room do I stop watching. Every night before a show he comes into my dressing room and together we do a warm-up, just to stretch the vocal cords. I do my best to be loud and goofy, improvising lyrics, acting boisterous and loud. Tonight we sing the Beatles 'I Saw Her Standing There', with a brash, deliberately off-key ending that could break glass.

Someone asks me what I'd like to eat later, when I'm on the tour bus. After the show, the guys in the band are often hungry and look forward to burgers or dim sum, which an assistant has waiting for us. I'm eating healthy while on tour, so I'm having cottage cheese and fruit.

I'm dressed and ready for the stage, but I take a few minutes to play ping-pong. The ping-pong table is custom-made and goes with me everywhere. It's kept conveniently close to the stage entrance so that I can play a bit before I head on to the stage. I love ping-pong. You might say I'm addicted to it. I have such a large crew that there's always somebody to play with, which makes me feel like I'm at summer camp.

I bat the ball back and forth, then head through a heavy curtain into the darkness of the immediate backstage area. I can hear the collective din of thousands of people and then a sound guy puts my ear monitors in. I punch fists with the group of handlers around me, a little pre-show ritual of mine. Then I turn and run up the stairs that take me to the stage. I wait for my cue, go through the curtain, slide down the raked stage platform and on to the stage. I launch into the big, bombastic, over-the-top 'Cry Me A River', and the crowd goes nuts. I'm a kid again. Every night, it's nothing short of thrilling.

Since the beginning, I've made a point of going into the audience and interacting with the crowds. I love to see their faces, to make them happy. With the *Crazy Love* show, I go out to Stage B, which is in the middle of the audience, with my opening a cappella act Naturally 7, who, as you know, sing back-up on some of my songs. As I walk through the audience, I'm accompanied by a burly bodyguard, but not because I think I'm a big shot. As I said before, there was an incident where a delusional man tried to attack me. Walking through a crowd of strangers, even seemingly happy ones, can have its risks. Mind you, I've more often witnessed violence than been on the receiving end of it. I once saw a lady punch another lady in the face at a show in France because one was blocking the other's view. It turned into a brawl, and my sister happened to be at that show in the eighth row. In that moment we locked eyes. She looked terrified.

More recently, a lady who'd perhaps had too much to drink got up on the B-stage, which is a small stage I go to for part of my show and is set up among the audience. She proceeded to fall off it. It was a six-foot drop and she hit the floor hard. I was so shocked I didn't know what to say, but as soon as I was sure she wasn't hurt, I looked at the camera and said, 'I pushed her.' That's me trying to make light of an awkward situation.

Back on the tour bus after the show, I'm slumped on a leather couch staring at the big screen TV, basking in the Vancouver three–nil win over Chicago. I'm already formulating how to work Vancouver's win into my opening at the Chicago show the next day. I share my tour bus with my assistant Holly and three of my musicians – piano player Alan Chang, sax player Jacob Rodriguez and trombone player Nick Vayenas. I have a bedroom with a queen-size bed and private washroom at the back of the bus, while everybody else sleeps in a separate compartment on bunk beds, like you would on a train. In the living area, we often stay up till the wee hours of the morning, playing Wii golf and baseball games. After a show, I'm often too wound up to sleep. And, besides, when you're living in a cocoon, what does it matter what time you go to bed?

While I was performing, Holly decorated the bus interior with Christmas ornaments and lights to remind us that Christmas is only a few weeks away. I met Holly after I'd just gone through a major break-up and, to make matters worse, my favourite stylist had quit. She was living in her homeland, Australia, and she'd never even been to North America when she came to work for me. She was supposed to be a fill-in stylist, but ended up staying on as both stylist and personal assistant. She shops for my clothes, she cuts my hair, she orders my food, my medications, my Christmas cards, you name it. She organizes my life, and now Lu's, even when we're on holiday. I'm almost reluctant to call Holly my assistant, because she's far more than that. She's become a great friend, and I regard her more as a little sister than an employee.

By morning, I've decided to give the Chicago audience a major drubbing for the Vancouver win. I'll do it in the most backhanded way possible. I'll congratulate them on winning the Stanley Cup while a huge image on the screen behind me flashes the three–nil score for Vancouver. I discuss the idea with one of my crew guys, then call my dad to talk about Christmas bonuses for the crew. My dad is one of my closest advisers. I have a loyal crew, many of whom have worked with me for seven years, and I believe in treating people well. A caterer travels with us and prepares healthy, delicious food for everyone. There is also a gym set up in case anyone feels the need to work out. And at Christmas, I give generous bonuses because, as my dad says, if you give people peanuts, you get monkeys working for you. In other words, you get what you pay for.

After a long dark drive through a blizzard, we arrive in a winter wonderland in Chicago. The bus drives underground, we all trundle into the backstage bunker and I follow the signs to my dressing room. There are a dozen other trucks and buses travelling with me, and the crew always arrives to set up first.

In my dressing room there are signs that Chicago is very much a hockey town. I see a stack of hockey memorabilia gifts from fans, including a Blackhawks jersey with my name on it. There is also a stack of CDs. I spend about an hour signing them before the show for the merchandise table, because I think it's a nice touch for fans.

I'm at my dressing-table and I'm thinking back to the old days, when I was desperate to get on a local radio programme to be heard by around a thousand people. I remember those days so clearly, working so hard to be heard by so few. It astounds me that I now play to audiences of fifty thousand people, as I did in Ireland last year, or multiple nights to sold-out audiences in Madison Square Garden.

Holly says she's not feeling well; she's a little tired. We've been without a break for several months, and the crew is starting to feel it too.

I take out my journal and make my daily entry. I like to keep track of my thoughts and experiences, and I often share them with Lu, to keep connected. She's at my house in Los Angeles with her mother, waiting for me to join them when the tour brings me there in a couple of weeks. I'll be playing Staples Center and also performing on the *Tonight Show with Jay Leno*. Most importantly, I'll get to see Lu again. Before that, I have a few more days on the tour bus and then I fly to New York for the annual Christmas concert, Jingle Ball Rock, to perform alongside artists like Katy Perry and Justin Bieber. I'll then fly from New York to Los Angeles. The band and crew will stay at hotels while I'll be at my house. When we're not on the tour bus, we're in hotels.

Because my life has slid into a repetitive cycle of recordings, promotion and touring, time is slipping away. The last seven years have sped by. It scares me; it makes me wonder if the next seven years will go as quickly. I want to slow it down, to savour it. I want to live in the present. By keeping a journal, I feel I'm doing that in a way, keeping the details alive so I'll experience them as they happen.

My life looks like this:

white hotel sheets that smell like laundry
room service menus, small soaps
dressing-room tables with my laptop, deodorant, water bottles
round dining tables littered with celebrity magazines
production desks in generic grey windowless rooms
coloured-paper signs on dressing-room doors with my name in felt pen
paper schedules posted on walls everywhere

my life now

a black ping-pong table and pink balls
backstage fluorescent lights, grey concrete
my ever-present BlackBerry and iPhone

The rooms are nondescript, a temporary refuge for a bunch of transients. My name and face, it seems, are everywhere. People wear laminates with my face on them. There are big posters backstage with my face, my name.

The equipment cases have my name on the side, as do the schedules posted on the walls. The merchandise table, too. It's a weird thing, being famous. People look at me and do one of two things. They either smile at me, like I'm a long-lost friend, or pretend they're not impressed, even though they kind of are. I like to tease people about it too, like this girl one time at a movie theatre who acted really nonchalant when I paid for my ticket. But once I got inside and was standing at the candy counter, I could hear her screaming over the walkie-talkies that all the staff were wearing, 'Oh, my God, Michael Bublé just walked in!'

I laughed. I made sure she got tickets to my show that night and then I proceeded to tease her about it from the stage.

Backstage, I get around on a Segway, the two-wheeled, self-balancing contraption on which I ride standing up. I have several backstage so that my crew can go from A to B quickly if they need to. For example, backstage in Chicago, I whip along on my Segway from the catering room to the ping-pong table for a quick game with Roger Thomas from Naturally 7. I like to tease him that I'll always beat him, and he plays along. When I finish playing ping-pong, I whip back to my dressing room to get ready for an interview with a British TV host. He's presenting me with a plaque for *Crazy Love* selling two million copies in the UK. Holly does my makeup, and I wear some nice casual jeans and a blue sweater. The TV host does a Sean Connery impression: 'Michael Bublé, I like your music, but that jumper has to go.' Everybody in the room laughs. We get into a lot more ribbing, lots of chuckles and goofing around. I can't help it. I'm a goofball when there's a TV camera around.

As I said, I consider myself more of an entertainer than a singer, an old-time variety act that combines song with comedy. There aren't too many entertainers out there doing a hybrid act like mine, and I think it gives the audience a way better experience than merely listening to me sing my way through a set list. I write a lot of my own jokes, often off the top of my head, but I also have comedian friends who write jokes for me. I've even hired the writers from Jay Leno's show. I'm good friends with a lot of comedians, such as Canadian comic Russell Peters and British comic Peter Kay. Russell has a great self-deprecating sense of humour. I learn a lot just by watching and hanging out with him. When

I'm in England, I hang out a lot with Peter, another hilarious guy who's taught me a lot about comedy and timing, and life in general.

In Chicago, I do a sound check with a bunch of contest winners. I sing for them and ask them questions. I tease a guy about the age difference between himself and his fiancée. He looks old enough to be engaged to her mother, who's also there. Afterwards I do a 'meet and greet' with the sponsor, Beringer Wines. I tell them a funny story about how I took some Ambien, which is a mild sedative, and went swimming with turtles in Hawaii. The story is ridiculous, but they laugh. Almost everybody is so sweet to me backstage. Even a representative from Warner visits me with a scrapbook of photos of me she's taken over the years.

The show goes without a hitch. The joke I wrote about the hockey game for the Chicago audience goes over well. Later, I'm lounging on my bed in the back of my tour bus and some of my band mates are up front, drinking beers and kicking back. I can hear them laughing. I don't party much on the road because I like to be in top form to sing every night. I no longer need booze, potato chips and cigarettes to sedate me after the show. I do, however, need Lu. I phone her constantly. No wonder my cell-phone bill is over the top.

As I lie on the bed, my feet are in a massage machine that squeezes them like bread dough. There's nothing personal in this room. It's just another room on another tour bus. I've got some of my clothes strewn about, but the vibe is temporary, like so many of the sleeping rooms I pass through all year long. In the corner, swaying on a hook is one of my suits, a Hugo Boss. I think about my first suit, given to me by my grandpa. It didn't fit well, not like the ones I wear these days, but it was the only suit I had, and I wore it everywhere. I think about how I'll see my grandpa soon back home in Vancouver. He's also planning to visit me in Australia. He is still my number-one supporter.

If there's one thing I've done right, it's keeping the important people in life close to me. I've got great family, friends and professional relationships.

I've surrounded myself with talented people who have helped me become more talented too. Some of the people around me say that that is one of my strengths, knowing who to go to for advice and support. Those people include Bruce and my producers Bob Rock, Humberto Gatica and David Foster, and too many others to list here.

After the Christmas break, I spent January starting to make a Christmas record with David, Humberto and Bob in Los Angeles. I'd wanted to make a Christmas album for eight years. By February, I'd be back on the road in Australia, and after that I'd be getting married, so I had to squeeze the recording around my schedule. I planned on returning to the studio in July.

my life now

I'd been thinking of songs and was firm about keeping them traditional. David has a policy about Christmas albums, that they should always be covers of the classics, and this is coming from a guy who wrote a widely covered original Christmas tune called 'Grown Up Christmas List'. But even he pushed for the old tunes. I agree with David. There are things that you don't mess with. I grew up listening to Bing Crosby's *Merry Christmas* album, and I dream that my kids will one day listen to mine. I wanted to capture the same warmth and charm of those old albums of yesteryear.

I also pushed again to keep the music recorded live, the old-school way. And I mean really live, like the way Frank and Bing and Dean did it, not the so-called live recording where you sing it live, then fix everything afterwards. I envisaged 'Silent Night' with only harp and quartet, nothing more. I wanted it beautiful, rich and authentic, without Pro Tools or any fancy technology. As my piano player Alan says, if you use acoustic instruments that you can't plug in, the sound becomes timeless. Anyone who has listened to a 1980s band that was heavy on the synthesizers knows what it means to sound dated.

David likes to describe the sound as a 'beautiful warm sweater wrapped around you', which is a pretty perfect way to sum it up. He said, 'You're the only guy around right now who can deliver a sound like this,' which made me feel pretty good.

I could have gone into the studio and sung along to twelve tracks arranged and produced someone else's way, but that's no longer how I operate. I'd rather spend a lot of time and money on doing it the right way. It can cost around $150,000 a day to record like this, but for me, it's about artistic integrity. I sing live with an orchestra, without headphones on. I sing better when I'm not wearing headphones.

Christmas is my favourite time of the year, and I cannot wait to promote that album, to sing all those songs on TV shows. A couple of months later, I found out I'd won my third Grammy, for *Crazy Love*. I'd previously won for my album *Call Me Irresponsible* and for my live 2009 release, *Michael Bublé Meets Madison Square Garden*. Along with the other two, I gave my third Grammy to my manager, Bruce, to display in his office.

As for what's next, I'm still writing songs and reading scripts that come my way. I have always loved all aspects of the entertainment industry, even though I'm a singer at heart. As for my personal life, Lu and I want to start a family, we want to pursue our careers, we want to divide our time between Argentina and North America. We'll continue to give to charities, including the formation of an animal shelter Lu wants us to launch in Argentina. The welfare of animals is close to her heart. She brings her little dog Simon with her everywhere. I am co-owner of the Vancouver Giants hockey team, which includes a box at the arena for patients at the local children's hospital, for which I am spokesman. I love kids, and couldn't imagine the pain of having a sick child. I long to see my own children play backstage, where Lu and I will set up jungle gyms and toys and do our best to keep the family together even while we work and travel.

Although you can never know where life will take you, I've had a plan in my head that I've somehow managed to follow. In an interview back in 2007, I told a reporter friend that I envisaged getting married within five years, starting a family, playing a few film roles, wearing the music producer's hat. I've since married Lu and am making inroads on those other plans, so I'm a happy guy.

All my life I felt too insecure to do a lot of things. For so long, I struggled against invisible demons. I felt restless and didn't know why. I've never felt academically smart, but I knew I had a different kind of intelligence. I didn't know business but I understood it. It's been that way with a lot of things. I have an instinct for what works. My life changed when I became a professional singer. I found my purpose and my calling. I started to see the potential in myself, and it was easier to wake up in the morning. When I started to work at this career, I started to find my happiness. I had something to live for. I wasn't so scared any more.

I still feel like I'm just getting started. There is a lot more I want to do. But at the end of the day, when the autographs are signed and the crowds have gone away, it all comes back to watching hockey with my sisters, eating a bowl of my grandma's red risotto with round steak, and uploading music on to my grandpa's iPod. In other words, I might have finally realized the career I'd always dreamed of, but I discovered along the way that I'll for ever be a Bublé – that dorky kid from Burnaby, writing songs on his dad's fishing boat.

photographs

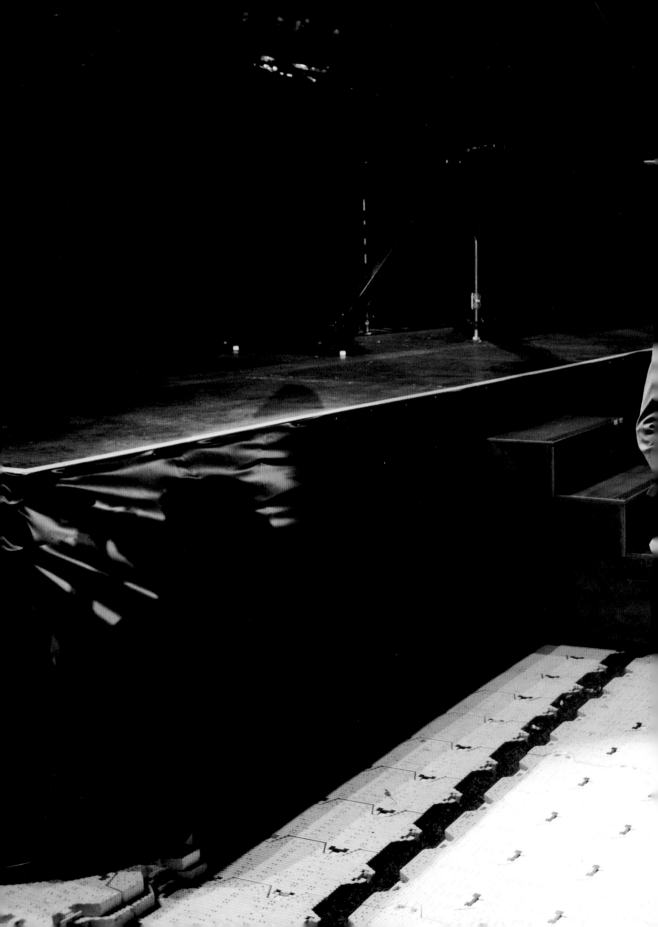

NOTTINGHAM, ENGLAND

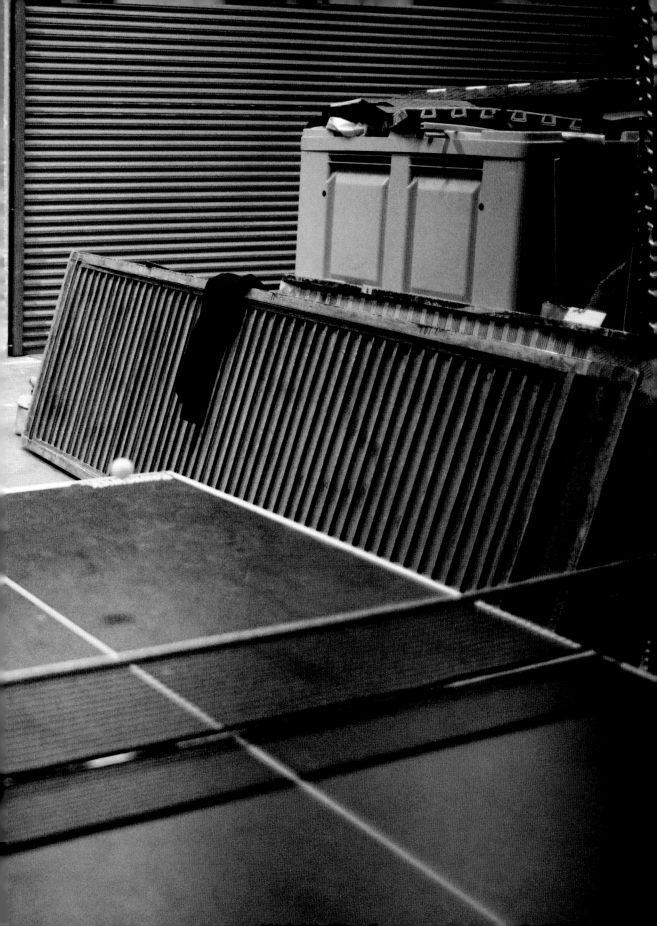

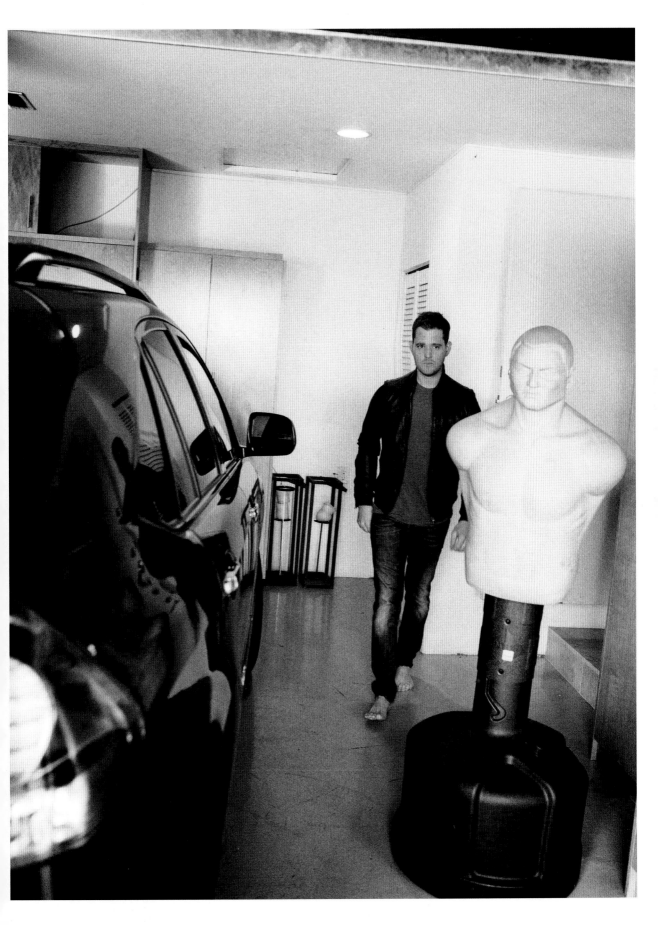

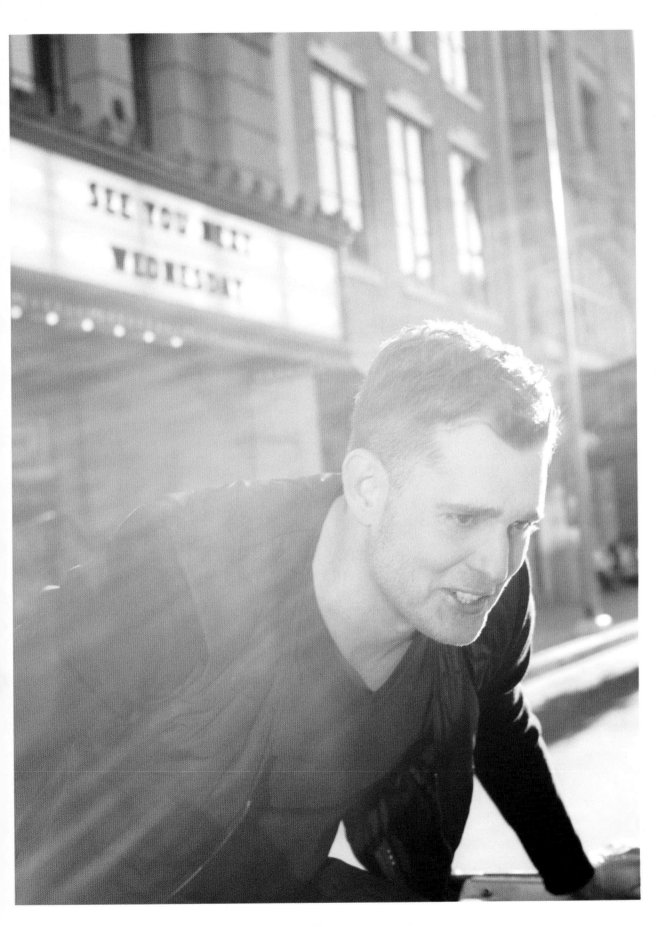

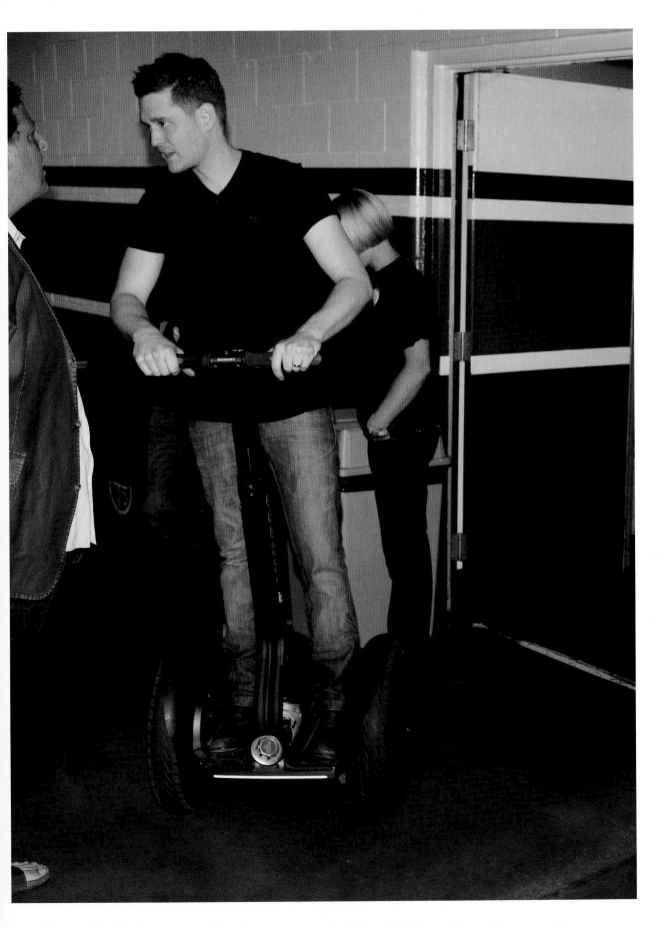

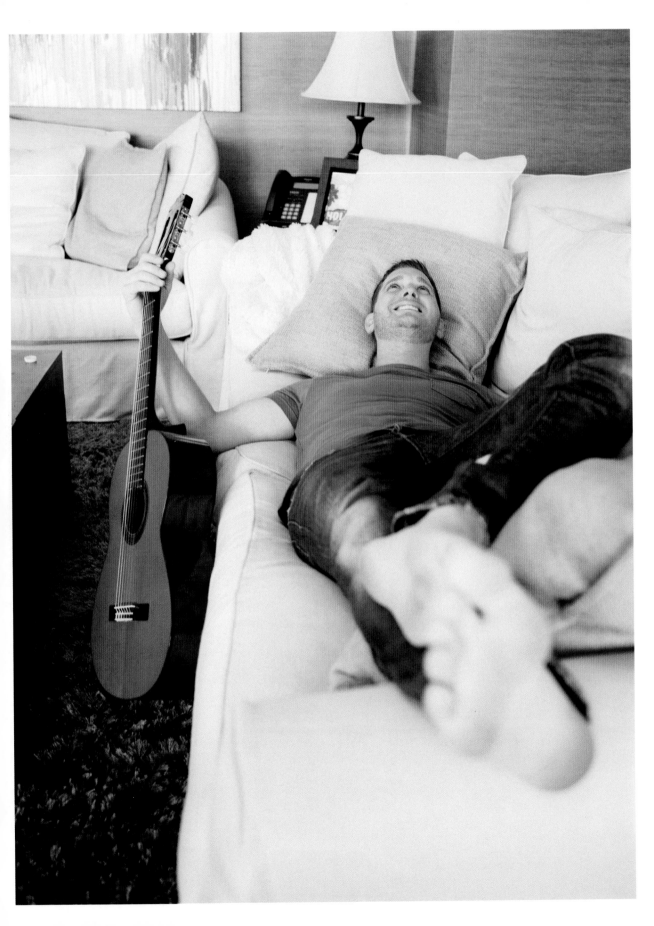

index of photographs

82–83

84–85

86–87

88–89

90–91

92–93

94–95

96–97

98–99

100–101

102–103

104–105

82–83
On the Hollywood video set, Universal City,
California

88–89
London, Wembley Arena, dressing room: three
minutes to show time

94–95
With Bruce Allen, manager, on route to LA

100–101
Notting Hil, London

84–85
Portobello Road, London, a day off on tour

90–91
Hollywood video set with extras

96–97
Front of stage Dublin

102–103
Dublin's Aviva stadium

86–87
Vancouver, Rogers Arena

92–93
Recording Christmas album at the world-famous
Capitol Studios, Hollywood

98–99
My Hollywood house, and show time

104–105
My pool in Hollywood

106-107

108-109

110-111

112–113

114–115

116–117

118–119

120–121

122–123

124–125

126–127

128–129

106–107
Backstage after Dublin stadium show

112–113
Showtime, and with Holly Russell at the Beringer Winery, Napa, California

118–119
Backstage in Dublin

124–125
Napa Valley: getting off private jet, and Beringer Winery

108–109
Backstage at Rogers Arena with Grandpa and Grandma

114–115
With Bob Rock and and team at Capitol Studios recording session

120–121
My pool in Hollywood

126–127
Someone has to take the trash out

110–111
The gates to my Hollywood house

116–117
On the Hollywood video set (spaceman), and downtime in Napa

122–123
With my two brothers-in-law, Rob (back seat), Lanny (driving) and best friend Carsten Love (shotgun), Hollywood video set

128–129
With David Foster at Capitol Studios

130–131

132–133

134–135

136–137

138–139

140–141

142–143

144–145

146–147

148–149

150–151

152–153

130–131
At home with Luisana in Hollywood

136–137
With my buddy Carsten, and Rob and Lanny

142–143
In my backyard at my Vancouver house

148–149
Getting through the crowd to B stage at Dublin Aviva stadium can be scary

132–133
London, and Dublin

138–139
Capitol Studios, Hollywood, and Portobello Road, London

144–145
Playing around the pool at home in Vancouver

150–151
With Jose (security) and Holly (PA and stylist)

134–135
With my dad Lewis and Bruce Allen at dinner in Vancouver

140–141
Me and Grandpa wine tasting at Beringer Winery (Yes, Grandpa is having some makeup put on), and Nottingham on stage

146–147
Luisana decides to throw me in the pool

152–153
Dressing room, Manchester: last night of the run

154–155

156–157

158–159

160–161

162–163

164–165

166–167

168–169

170–171

172–173

174–175

176–177

154–155
Dublin Aviva stadium

160–161
New York

166–167
In motorhome on break on the Hollywood video shoot

172–173
Arriving at the Rogers Arena with Lusiana

156–157
On my tour bus: this is my bedroom on the road

162–163
On the B stage at Dublin, and London

168–169
On stage, Nottingham, England

174–175
On private jet, with Jo Faloona, Holly Russell and Mitra Darab

158–159
With amazingly funny comedian and friend Peter Kay in Manchester

164–165
Hanging out on break, Hollywood video set

170–171
With backing singers at Capitol Studios

176–177
Muscle car: some cool shots on break, Universal City, California

178–179

180–181

182–183

184–185

186–187

188–189

190–191

192–193

194–195

196–197

198–199

200–201

202–203

204–205

206–207

208–209

210–211

212–213

214–215

216–217

218–219

220–221

222–223

224–225

202–203
Onstage and at home in Hollywood

208–209
Onstage and at home in Vancouver

214–215
London hotel on tour, and at home in Vancouver
with Luisana

220–221
Soundcheck on the B stage, Dublin Aviva stadium

204–205
Pool-time, Hollywood, and Ice hockey in
Nottingham, UK

210–211
Jo Faloona (Marketing at Bruce Allen Talent)
Napa valley, California

216–217
Backlot break on video shoot

222–223
Hollywood video set

206–207
A break on the Hollywood video set

212–213
Table tennis backstage

218–219
With ice hockey team in Nottingham, UK

224–225
Beringer vineyard in Napa, California

226–227

228–229

230–231

232–233

234–235

236–237

238–239

240–241

242–243

244–245

246–247

248–249

226–227
On my Vespa in Vancouver with Luisana

232–233
Hollywood video

238–239
In my hotel suite on tour, London

244–245
David Foster recording session with the choir

228v229
On stage

234–235
Backstage, and one of my characters on the Hollywood video

240–241
With producer David Foster, and at my Hollywood house

246–247
With Bob Rock

230–231
At home in Vancouver

236–237
On the B stage at Wembley Arena, London

242–243
Portobello Road, London

248–249
Holly Russell getting me ready before a show

250–251

252–253

254–255

256–257

258–259

260–261

262–263

264–265

266–267

268–269

270–271

272–273

250–251
Hollywood video set

256–257
Walking to stage, Vancouver, with Bruce Allen, Don Fox and Jose Martini

262–263
As above

268–269
Vancouver, and with Naturally 7 on B stage

252–253
On my Segway backstage in Vancouver

258–259
Hollywood video (impersonating Justin Bieber), me and Luisana in my dressing room, Vancouver

264–265
James Dean, and on private jet

270–271
Hollywood video set

254–255
Beringer Winery, and on break on video shoot

260–261
Notting Hill, London, and Napa, California

266–267
Hollywood pool, and Capitol Studios

272–273
With Luisana and Dino Meneghin in my dressing room, Vancouver

274–275

276–277

278–279

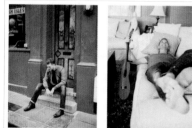
280–281

282–283

284–285

286–287

288–289

274–275
Vancouver

276–277
Dublin sound check, and at home in Hollywood

278–279
At home in Hollywood

280–281
Notting Hill, London, and at home in Hollywood

282–283
Going back on stage, Dublin Aviva stadium, Jose Martini, security

284–285
Holly cutting my hair, and with Luisana in Vancouver

286–287
Press conference, Rogers Arena, Vancouver

288–289
Wembley Arena, London

dean freeman biography

Over the past fifteen years, Dean Freeman has mastered the genre of celebrity documentation, producing over ten books, many of them global bestsellers, for which he acts not only as the sole photographer, but also as the creative director and publishing consultant.

His signature style is inspired by the Hollywood glamour of the 1950s and 1960s, transposed to the twenty-first century and made to feel 100 per cent now.

Dean's books are often imitated and yet none of these imitations offer the same richness and depth of imagery, combined with the design and overall quality of publications Dean intricately masterminds.

Dean's photographs are beautiful, fun, dynamic, honest and warm, and his character and subtle approach gain the trust of stars and enable him to bring to the world unique portraits of these modern icons who rarely allow such intimate coverage.

This is a testament to the man and his talent responsible for icon-making in the most truthful and artistic way. Dean is simply a master, one of the world's preeminent photographers and publishing visionaries in this genre.

Michael with Dean

Part of the charm of these books is that he makes the images seem so effortless. This is far from the truth: Dean's ability to seize a moment and still flatter his subject is a truly magical skill.

thank you

I would like to thank Michael for being a dream subject and collaborator. Michael is one of the warmest and most talented stars I have had the pleasure to work with in over two decades.

He is a true voice of an angel and, at the same time, an inimitable, charismatic performer who fills theatres and stadiums worldwide with his unassuming attitude and natural, irresistible charm.

It is an honour to have been allowed into the Bublé world and the warmth and affection of his family and management are truly unique and will stay in my heart. I would also like to thank Michael's beautiful wife Luisana and all of the Bublé family, especially the 'Granddad', Mitch, and Lewis Bublé.

Thank you to Bruce Allen, firstly for often calling me 'kiddo' and mostly for sharing the vision and the trust and support in getting this book finished. A genuinely amazing man, manager, legend.

Thank you to Jo Faloona, a real star behind the scenes. Holly Russell, what can I say? This girl is a force of nature and simply this book would not have been possible without the amazing talent of Michael's right-hand woman.

To all the tour management, especially Chris Chappel, band and crew, thank you for your assistance. And, of course, the guardian angel Jose, gentle and tough. To Doug Young and Transworld: great team and great vision. Dion the Singer, Susan Leon and Mitra Darab, Carsten Love, Chris Fussell, Tory Class, Alan Chang, Bob Rock, David Foster: it has been a pleasure to meet you.

Thank you to Joby Ellis, design backbone and talent. To Richard Poulton, digital genuis. Chris Organ, legal legend and Ryan Vince at *Russell's*. To David Lyons and Toby Dodson for LA support. A big Abraco to my Canadian buddy Michael Chamberlain and LPB you're a star.

Love to my amazing wife Olga and son Dylan. You are my world.

thank
you

Believe it or not, I'm not a fan of getting my picture taken. So when I get comfortable with a photographer, it makes the procedure a little easier to handle. Dean Freeman is not only a great photographer, he has the innate ability not to invade one's space. To get the photos he's looking for, that skill is paramount. Dean, I thoroughly enjoyed working with you. You are a true gentleman. I'm glad I've had the chance to get to know you and I look forward to hanging with you for years to come.

To Lu – my wife. Thank God you are used to this . . . And gawd you're hot!

Thank you to Holly, my tireless assistant, who has to cope with an incredibly busy schedule. Somehow it all gets done – thanks to her dedication and skill.

Thanks to Jo Faloona for her calendar manipulations. I hate that calendar. Just kidding!

A special thanks to Kerry Gold. Without her, this book didn't have a ghost of a chance of coming to fruition.

Thanks to my wonderful family and my incredible friends. My band and crew – who I consider my brothers and sisters. This journey wouldn't have been half as sweet without you.

Okay, Bruce! You were right. Thanks for talking me into it.

To all my fans – I hope you enjoy it!

Michael Bublé